My Life My Story

Iris Edith Madden

Grosvenor House
Publishing Limited

This book is published by
Grosvenor House Publishing Ltd
Link House
140 The Broadway, Tolworth, Surrey, KT6 7HT.
www.grosvenorhousepublishing.co.uk

A CIP record for this book
is available from the British Library

ISBN 978-1-78623-173-4

Disclaimer

This book is a memoir. It reflects the author's recollections of experiences over time. Some names have been changed or omitted, some events have been compressed. But the author has done her best to tell a truthful story by using many documents to support it.

Acknowledgments

My life would have been very different if my Mum, Mary Alice Holbrey hadn't fostered me. She nurtured me throughout my childhood and taught me the values of kindness, generosity and being respectful. Although no longer with us in body to her I say;

There I sat lonely and afraid.
You got a call and came to my aid.
You bundled me with blankets and love.
And when I needed it most, you gave me a hug.
I learned that the world is not all that scary and cold.
That sometimes there is someone to have and to hold.
You taught me what love is you helped me to mend.
You loved me and healed me and became my first friend.

My Dad, my brother Ronnie and his wife Sheila you have played an important role in my life since being a small child. I thankyou from the bottom of my heart for everything you have done for me.

To my extended foster family of Grandparents, Aunties, Uncles and Cousins you also played a vital role in that you accepted me as 'one of the family' and played a vital part of my childhood and made many happy memories for me. Thankyou all for being you.

To my birth siblings; John, Shirley, Ken, Maggie, May, Irene, Tommy and Robert I am proud of you all for the people who you have become and am pleased we are always there for each other.

Without my friends in particular; David, Jennifer, Ian, Fran, Brian, Judith, Sylvia, Pat, Marie, Janet and Allyson the darkest days would have been even darker. You have my heartfelt thanks for the support that you have given to me and my children.

Special thanks to Merryn and Emma for proof reading my book

The greatest achievement in life are my four children; Melissa, Daniel, Andrew and Hannah. I love each of you unconditionally as a mother should. You are my pride and joy.

Lastly my husband Mike, you have shown me what true love is and all that it encompasses, there is no greater gift. Thank you for that and all the support that you have given me in everything I do for me especially when I have been writing this book.

Chapter One

Hello World

I arrived into the world at midday on Sunday 3rd February 1957. I was born at home it was usual to be born at home then. My home was 6 Carlisle Terrace, Dinnington, Sheffield, Yorkshire. The house is still there, it is a mid-terraced house just off the High Street in Dinnington. My birth parents and older sister, May lived in one of the upstairs rooms, the house was rented by an old lady who lived downstairs. I have no recollection of this momentous event and only recently discovered my birth weight was 7lb 4oz. I have never seen a photo of myself as a baby. The reason for this is that I became what is now called a 'looked after child'. I was given the names Iris Edith, my first name being the same as my birth mother's sister and my second name being the same as my birth father's mother and one of his sisters. This book will inform you about my journey from birth to present. Finding out the truth about why I was taken into care and the interesting but traumatic path my life has followed.

As a child I liked the fact that I was born on a Sunday due to the rhyme;

Monday's child is fair of face.
Tuesday's child is full of grace.
Wednesday's child is full of woe.
Thursday's child has far to go.
Friday's child works hard for a living.
Saturday's child is loving and giving.
But the child that is born on the
Sabbath is bonny, blithe, good and gay.

I believed that I should be good and happy because the rhyme said that I was. The rhyme was in a children's book that I was given as a birthday present.

I love the fact that I am a Yorkshire lass in fact I am very proud of that. Some people try and mimic and belittle Yorkshire people to the extent of trying by attempting to mimic a Yorkshire accent in such a way that it insinuates that Yorkshire people are stupid. They haven't a clue that someone born in South Yorkshire will have a dialect different to those in West Yorkshire, North Yorkshire or East Yorkshire and even within those areas there will be differences. For instance, my brother says water as in w a (as in apple) t e r whereas I say water as in war ter. Am I a posh Yorkshire lass? or is it due to being chastised for saying w a (as in apple) ter. I don't say thee and tha either. However, I don't mind the colloquialism used by any of my Yorkshire peers I feel at home when I hear the accent. I love Yorkshire and most people born in Yorkshire would agree. Or maybe I feel that way because I feel that I 'belong' there.

 My earliest memories are of living in Oakwood Grange Children's Home, Rotherham. Most of us will have flashbacks to being a very young child, to events that had such an impact on us in our earliest years that we remember them forever. It seems strange in some ways that I have no recollection of being taken away from my birth parents but then again, I was only two years old. My sister May who is 18 months older than me does remember it. She has informed me that we were in a big black car sitting together on the back seat, that I was crying and trying to stand up, she told me that she had tried to reassure me and said, 'it's okay I will look after you and we will be better off'. Quite a statement to make considering she was only four years old. Maybe she had heard an adult say that we would be better off in care than with our birth parents. May, remembers a lady sitting on the front seat holding a baby. When giving some thought to that it must have been Tommy our younger brother at that moment in time and it was confirmed years later that it was him. May doesn't have any recollection of our younger sister Irene being in the car with us but we have since discovered that Irene had initially been taken into Lodge Moor Hospital before being taken to Oakwood Grange. In Oakwood Grange however, we would not have had day to day contact with Irene as she was younger than us and would have been placed in the nursery as was Tommy. May and I were therefore separated from our younger two siblings on the point of being taken into care.

Oakwood Grange was where Rotherham District Hospital now stands. There was a long drive with trees lining it leading up to the house. The drive was next to what was the grammar school. Years later when I was living in Teesside I became friends with two men who had grown up in Rotherham and attended that school at around the time I was there, it is a small world. Oakwood Grange was a large Victorian house that had been turned into a children's home. The house was made of stone, the front of the house had large windows and a large wooden and glass front door. Inside the house some of the floors were tiled and some were wooden so whenever anyone walked or ran around you could hear the noise echo around. The house always smelled of polish and cleaning products, it was well looked after by the staff. I remember the house and grounds very well and it was a great shame when the main house was knocked down to make way for Rotherham District Hospital and its car park.

There was a large fenced off area in the grounds. I frequently climbed up the fence to try and get the donkey who lived on the other side of the fence to come over so that I could stroke it. The elderly man who looked after the donkey and the grounds would talk to me and the other children and he would encourage us not to be frightened of the donkey. People who know me now might not believe it, but I didn't say very much to the man in fact I didn't say very much to anyone at all as I was very shy but would overcome my shyness so that I could stroke the donkey.

My other memories of the time when I lived at Oakwood Grange include sleeping in a white metal bed on wheels, similar to those found in hospitals during that time. The beds were around the sides of a large room and other children slept in those beds. May's bed was next to mine, where else would she be? May looked after me as she had said she would when we were in the car. We always played together, when the weather was fine we frequently played outside in the grounds where we ran around as children do with the other children. I can remember May often pushing me around on a sit and ride toy. It was a large dog on wheels, you see them in museums now, even though I couldn't push her on it she spent ages pushing me around on it. I can remember one of the adults on occasions pushing May around on it so that she could have her turn.

There are some moments during the time that I lived in Oakwood Grange that frightened me enormously and had an impact on me for years. On one occasion I remember being lined up with other children in a large stone flagged scullery that had large rectangular white pot sinks. This room was quite dark as it had quite small windows. As I waited in line I could see a man who was wearing a white coat. I could hear that he had quite a deep voice and noticed that when the individual children went up to him he made them cry. Due to lining up and watching all the other children getting upset, when it got to my turn I had become really tense and frightened and yes, I did cry in fact I screamed when he stuck something sharp in my arm, it really hurt. This was my first experience of having injections. I still don't like injections, but I am very brave and don't scream or cry anymore but it took me a very long time to become brave. There was no Mum to comfort any of us. It was like a mass programme of injections up you went, he stabbed you with the needle you cried and then you were quickly moved out of the way ready for the next child to be stabbed. I wonder if they did this to their own children, why didn't one of the members of staff sit the individual children on their knee give some reassurance and cuddle them before and after they had been vaccinated. Looking back, it seems very cold and impersonal. I know now with all the safeguarding of children it might be frowned upon for staff to cuddle a child, but I do know that in the special schools that I have worked in, the nurses and staff support and reassure any child who must have any treatment if the parent isn't able to be there to do it. When I took my own children for their injection's I made it as calm as I could make it and there were lots of cuddles afterwards. I didn't enjoy that part of motherhood at all and due to my apprehension about injections I was very tempted to persuade their Dad to take them but thought that I would be letting my children down. I was also told that I was being silly when I voiced my worries about taking them and that it would be fine. So sorry kids I did take you, but I did tell you what was going to happen and tried to reassure you before it happened that it would only hurt for a short time, sometimes you cried for a short time but not for too long and it was for your wellbeing. When I have seen the mass inoculation programmes of children in third world countries I have seen them line up but their mums or an adult are always there holding and comforting them.

Another scary moment that I remember is being taken a long walk with the other children, well it seemed a long walk to me as my legs were very small. We all wore the same outfits blue and white dresses for the girls and the boys in shirts and short trousers, it would like a school outing. It was a nice sunny day and all the children were running around or sitting on a grassy embankment. Suddenly there was lots of noise in the foreground it was a freight train there was a lot of very load banging and clanging from the train and what I now think was a steel works. I screamed and screamed in terror. May came to the rescue again and hugged me and tried to soothe me. None of the women who were in charge picked me up, hugged me or reassured me they were all sat around, and they just laughed and said not to be silly. Silly, for good-ness sake I was a terrified two-year-old. I needed a motherly figure not adults laughing at me.

The earliest memories I have of the lady who was to become my Mum; Mary Alice Holbrey, are of her being in our dormitory in Oakwood Grange, she was cleaning very early in the morning and chatting away to May. She was always a cheerful, smiling and friendly person and May of course would talk to anyone anyway and still does, in fact it is a struggle to get a word in most of the time! We both got to know her quite well and that was good for me as I was very quiet and shy at that time.

After a while I visited my home to be I remember the journey to visit my future Mum's home. I suppose that was because I had been confined to the boundaries of Oakwood Grange for months. Mum was a tall slim woman who always walked fast, especially for a little girl I remember her carrying me down a big hill and up another one, getting onto a big blue bus to travel to her house. Any direction from Oakwood Grange and from where Rotherham Hospital now stands you must go down a hill. Mum did tell me the way she walked with me years later after I informed her that I could remember going to her house for the first time. I had remembered it very well, we had crossed the main road and went down the steep hill and up the steep hill at the other side to Herringthorpe where we caught the bus. Mum was always watching the pennies and had worked out that it was cheaper catching the bus there rather than catching a bus into the town centre and then catching another one from the town centre to Maltby. Or she could have walked a long way into the town centre which was in the opposite direction to Maltby. So, the walk down the hill and then up a hill saved money and was going in the right direction for Maltby. I had a few weekend visits prior to me being fostered by my Mum and Dad to assess whether I would settle into the family. Apparently, I didn't say very much on these visits, but I wasn't frightened either.

I don't recall a moment when I went to live with my new family or feeling that I was being taken away from May, so it was obviously well organised and maybe as I didn't know any different I thought that it was normal and what people did. Mum was a lovely cheerful person who looked after me well when she took me to her home on weekend visits.

First, I should explain why Mum and Dad fostered me in more detail. My mum Mary Alice Holbrey was married to Clag (Clarence) they had a son eleven years older than me; Ronnie. When I was old enough to understand Mum explained to me that she had always wanted another child especially a daughter, but it had never happened, they had never been able to have another baby. In those days there wasn't all the knowledge there is available now about infertility, women either got pregnant or didn't. One of my older female cousins who lived around the corner from us when I went to live with Mum, Dad and Ronnie told me that she and her sisters had often been 'borrowed' by mum, she would put ribbons in their hair and do other mother daughter type activities.

Mum got a job working at Oakwood Grange as one of her friends, Miss Jones, who lived at the bottom of Dunns Dale, worked at Oakwood Grange Children's Home and after Miss Jones and Mum had a chat about Miss Jones' job and Mum saying that she wanted to work with children. When Miss Jones knew of a vacancy at Oakwood Grange, Mum applied for and got the job. Mum did other domestic duties there that included cleaning the room that May and I slept in. She would talk to the children and after a while Mum decided that she would like to foster a child, she chose me and for that I will always be eternally grateful to her for taking me into her home and her family and to my Dad and my brother Ronnie for accepting me into their lives too. By living with them I learnt what being part of a family was, how to treat people with respect along with good standards of hygiene. It was in part fate, being in the right place at the right time that I got the opportunity of a family life.

Ronnie appeared to have taken my arrival in his stride. Imagine being a fourteen-year-old boy, and even more importantly an only child having a three-year-old girl come and live with you. Even though I might have been a pest on very rare occasions I think I was also an asset as he got more freedom as Mum was very busy looking after me now to be chasing after him and what he was up to. I was quite a novelty with the teenage girls on the street too and Ronnie probably got a little more attention from them due to their interest in me.

I had lived in Oakwood Grange Children's Home for eight months by the time I was officially placed with my new family in a short-term foster placement. During that eight months May, Irene and I had not seen our birth parents at all and that was not the choice of social services, parents were actively encouraged to visit their children so that the children would not forget who their parents were and so that the parent/child bond would not be broken completely.

Chapter Two

New Beginnings

Having spent eight months living in Oakwood Grange Children's home together including Christmas, May and I were separated at the point we were placed in our foster homes. My foster Mum had wanted to foster both May and I to keep us together, but it had already been agreed that a Mr and Mrs Ellis who lived in Wath upon Dearne could foster May. Mrs Ellis was asked if she would relinquish May so that we could remain together, but she refused to do that. Irene had made visits to one of my foster Mum's sisters with a possibility of her and her husband fostering Irene but as they were moving away from Maltby due to my Mum's brother-in-law gaining employment in Derbyshire they were not allowed to foster Irene and therefore she was fostered at the same time as May and I to a Mr and Mrs Clarkson who lived in Bramley near Rotherham which was only a few miles from where I lived. Fortunately, all three foster mothers wanted May, Irene and I to have regular contact and wanted us to make visits to each other's foster homes on a frequent basis and social services agreed with this and as we were supposed to be in short term foster care and it was seen to be better therefore that we didn't forget each other. Tommy was no longer in care, he had been returned to our birth parents, we were told years later that it was thought by social services that our parents could cope with one baby. As I have stated our foster mums ensured that the three of us had regular contact, but our parents displayed no interest in us and through their own choice had very little contact with any of us whilst we were in care. They didn't even send letters or birthday cards to us which they could do through social services.

Mum, Dad, Ronnie and I lived in a typical three double bedroomed council house it was in a row of four, our house was one of the middle ones the one to the right of a gennel (a narrow tunnel also called a ginnel in some areas) between the two middle houses so that you could access the back of the two middle houses. The gennel was a great place to play especially if it was raining as I could continue to play outside with my friends. As I and my friends got bigger we could walk up the side walls of the gennel either with our back against one of the walls we were able to gradually move up with our feet on the other wall and using our hands to propel our bodies up the other wall or we would walk up the inside of the gennel by making our bodies into an x shape with a foot and hand on each wall. The aim was to touch the ceiling. I never achieved that but some of the taller children did. We got told off occasionally, if we played ball games in there as it must have echoed and the bang, bang, bang of the balls on the walls must have spoilt the sound of the radio programmes being listened to indoors. The elderly lady, Mrs Scholey who lived at the other side of the gennel never complained about the noise as we played but my Mum used to tell us to quieten down if we got too loud. The neighbours and the people living on the street were all lovely people and there was a real community spirit amongst the people living on the street and around Maltby, everyone knew everyone else and looked out for each other and back doors were really left open and wide open in the warmer weather!

Mr and Mrs Bratby our next-door neighbours had one of their grandsons living with them Ian, he was older than me. They held a bonfire and fireworks at their house on 5th November every year they had the end house and a huge garden at the side of their house as well as at the back of their house. Mrs Bratby, Mum and other ladies made jacket potatoes, bonfire toffee etc the big boys would have collected the wood for the bonfire for days before by dragging home branches of wood from the trees that were at the top of our street. Ronnie and his friends and spent hours down the woods, playing, climbing trees and messing about as did generations of children before them had done and I did with my friends. The boys oversaw the construction of the bonfire and the Dads and Mr Bratby would check it out and give their advice. All the families contributed fireworks. I was always very excited when Dad bought some fireworks for our contribution and I kept wanting to open the tin that they were kept in to have a look at them. Mum would keep saying 'Iris, leave those fireworks alone, they are dangerous'. They would be then put on a shelf high up out of my reach which was a good idea. On the day of the bonfire I would be very excited and keep pestering my Mum about when I could put my wellies, coat, gloves and hat on and go to

Mrs Bratby's house, but I don't know why as I liked the rockets and Catherine wheels but didn't like the bangers or the jumping jacks at all, they frightened me. The jumping jacks did just that, when they had been lit they jumped all over the floor and crackled spitting out sparks. To me they were out of control, so I used to run into the kitchen and look through the window at them but covered my ears up with my gloved hands until all the jumping jacks and bangers had finished. I liked the sparklers as well as the Catherine wheels and the fireworks that didn't bang and would write my name and make pretty patterns with the lit sparklers.

Mrs Bratby often popped into our house to see Mum and they would have a cup of tea and a gossip. Mum had lived in our house with her Mum and Dad when she was growing up and had sometimes looked after Mrs Bratby's children, so they had a very long and close friendship. Her first name was Minnie, but I wasn't allowed to call her that. When I was growing up and the way I was brought up it was very disrespectful to call an adult by their Christian name unless it had the prefix of Auntie or Uncle and Grandma and Grandad's were just that with the suffix of their surname if speaking about them to the children e.g. 'We are going to Grandma Hutchinson's or Grandad Hutchinson said....'. In their presence the children called them Grandma or Grandad.

At home during the day most women always wore a headscarf that was tied at the front above their foreheads and the ends of the scarf were tucked in. This was to keep their hair neat and tidy and not spoil the wash and set they had had done at the hairdressers, my mum always went on a Friday afternoon to get her hair done with a cut and a perm completed every six weeks or so. Women often had a roller or two in their fringes during the day especially if they were going out later. They wore slippers and their nylon stockings all day (there were no tights then) the stockings were rolled down to their ankles, so they wouldn't get laddered but would be quickly pulled up and connected to their suspender belts and the headscarf and rollers removed if someone knocked on the door. It took them seconds to do this as they were so skilled at it. They always wore their 'work clothes' with a flowery wraparound overall that had matching plain bias binding at the edges, the overall crossed over at the front and tied on the side over the top of their 'work clothes'. My Mum even had work shoes to do the housework in!

I often popped in to see our neighbour Mrs Scholey just to have a chat. I don't know how old Mrs Scholey was but she in my eyes she was very, very old. She was very small in stature and had short white hair and was in my eyes much older that Mrs Bratby! I thought she might be lonely as she lived on her own even though her family lived in Maltby and frequently popped in to see her and made sure that she was okay and had everything. Her Granddaughter Dorothy, who was a grown up in my eyes. I had been informed that she was training to be a teacher she would visit her Grandma often and used Mrs Scholey's sewing machine I was fascinated with this and spent hours chatting to her and watching what she did and asked her a lot of questions. I loved Mrs Scholey's house it was full of nick naks and framed photographs of her family, I never touched them though but loved looking at them. She had a very large framed photograph of her husband dressed in his army uniform on the wall that always had a poppy or two attached to it, he was a hero in my eyes. I especially loved visiting Mrs Scholey on a Monday morning as she had a huge boiler that she dragged out into the small passage between the kitchen door, coalhouse door and toilet door. She boiled all her white undies, towels and bedding in it. You could smell the washing powder from outside, and in the passage of her house you could feel the heat from the boiler and had to peer through the steam to see Mrs Scholey. Mrs Scholey also had a scrubbing board that she would use to scrub any marks on the clothing. She also had a poss stick, this was metal on one end and she held the stick and pushed the metal end up and down that created a suction to get the dirt from out of the items being washed. She wouldn't allow me to do this but would occasionally allowed me to use the wooden tongues to push the washing up and down gently if I was very careful as the water was boiling hot I felt very important doing this for Mrs Scholey. She also had dolly blues (little blue bags) that she put in the final rinse of her white's wash. Mrs Scholey told me that the little dolly blues made the whites continue to stay white. I was fascinated that something blue could make things whiter, but it did I checked Mrs Scholey's whites carefully.

Washday was just that a whole day due to the way it had to be done. No automatic washing machines or tumble dryers. Things were dried on the washing line outside or in front of the coal fire. As soon as they were dry enough they were ironed and put away after being aired. Aired means making sure they were no longer damp. When Mrs Scholey was ironing she used starch to make the table cloth and her dress and blouse collars and cuffs stiff. Mrs Scholey had a lovely kind face and was very patient with me asking her lots of questions. Mrs Scholey taught me how to do the washing properly, none of the automatic washers that we have nowadays. The washing and ironing took all day and the women seemed to be very satisfied with their efforts. Whites had to be sparkling white and the ladies would be checking each other's washing hung on their washing lines. It was quite an achievement I think as everyone had coal fires and there was a lot of soot around in the air. I like to think that I kept Mrs Scholey entertained and stopped her getting lonely. Mum wasn't very impressed when I started telling her about Mrs Scholey's underwear how big her knickers were and how long her vests were and told me that I shouldn't be looking or saying that. I also informed Mum all about how to do the washing properly, as if she didn't already know. Mrs Scholey bought me gifts at Christmas and one year she bought me a lovely fluffy yellow hat for Christmas it had a long yellow ribbon on it, I loved it and would have worn it in bed if I had been allowed. That hat is one of the things that I would have liked to have kept forever but I still remember Mrs Scholey well. I have very fond memories of both her and Mrs Bratby.

My Dad's Dad; Grandad Holbrey lived across the road from us and my Dads sister, Auntie Joan her husband; Uncle George and their family lived around the corner when I first moved in with my Mum. Dad and Ronnie. They had a big family Joanie, June, Joyce, Jean, Young

George and later Christopher. The post must have been a nightmare all those J Goodgroves living at the same address. The older girls were about Ronnie's age, young George was much younger than Ronnie but older than me. My new girl cousins used to play with me like a little sister, teaching me rhymes and games, I distinctly remember them teaching me amongst other things the rhyme 'Pop Goes the Weasel' when I was playing in their back garden, it took me a while to get the hang of making the popping noise with my finger and my cheek. Mum wasn't impressed when I was learning to do this as I repeatedly got spit all over my fingers when I was practising. Their younger brother Christopher was a couple of years younger than me, they moved around the time he was born to the other end of Maltby to a larger house. I missed them all when they moved but fortunately their new home was not too far away, so Mum and I used to visit them frequently. It was great when the girls got married they had fabulous family weddings with music and dancing. My Dad taught me how to waltz at these family weddings and do some country dancing such as the Gay Gordon's. Also, I could stay at the wedding reception until it finished which was very late at night. When he had had a few pints, my Dad used to sing and had a good singing voice, I loved to hear him sing, to me it meant that he was happy and not the beer making him happy as I didn't understand about the different effects that beer had on different people at that time.

My Dad had one sister, Auntie Joan and five brothers, Uncles Frank; Ken; Chuck (Charles); Horace and Fred. They were all married and had children of their own. Three of these uncles were in the Army and didn't live in

Maltby when I was growing up, but they would visit Maltby from time to time. The youngest brother Uncle Fred lived in Dinnington that wasn't too far from Maltby and was where I had been born. Uncle Fred married Auntie Gwen a few months after I had joined their family and I attended their wedding with my Mum, Dad and Ronnie. This wedding is another early memory that I have. A few days before the wedding Mum and I went to the newspaper shop in Maltby that also sold cards and other items. Mum bought some confetti and she and I also chose a pretty silver horseshoe. I didn't understand that I wouldn't be able to keep it and that it was to give to the bride to keep. After we came out of the church photographs were taken and Mum had already given me the horseshoe, so I had been holding the horseshoe for quite some time. Mum had a handbag I had a pretty horseshoe. Mum then took me up to the bride and groom to have my photo taken, that was okay but then I had to give the bride the horseshoe I was not allowed to keep it. Tears followed, and my eyes look puffy on the wedding photo. I have frequently asked for my horseshoe back and am still waiting for its return. It must have brought them luck as they have been married for almost sixty years. They did buy me a horseshoe when I was sixty which shows they appreciate the banter we have had about it. It has pride of place with other precious items on my sideboard.

My Mum had two brothers, Uncles Joe and Raymond and four sisters, Aunties Winnie, Edie, Norah and Doreen. They also had husbands and children. Uncles Joe and Raymond and Auntie Edie lived in other areas of England but would visit Maltby from time to time.

Auntie Doreen and her husband Uncle Ben lived else-where for a while but returned to Maltby. Mum and I would visit each of her sisters every week and my Dads Sister Auntie Joan, so we were quite a close-knit family. Every Christmas Day most of the relatives would meet up at Auntie Winnie's home for tea. The adults would be in the large kitchen/dining room and eat first the children of all ages would be in the front room playing games and would then eat after the adults had finished. It was always dark and cold when we walked back home. One Christmas I was ill, and we had to stay at home I think I was more upset about not going to Auntie Winnies than being ill and in discomfort.

My Mums parents; Grandma and Grandad Hutchinson lived in Maltby in a council house and we visited them a few times a week. They had a bird table and a sundial in their back garden that I was fascinated with and if there wasn't any water in the bird bath I would be allowed to fill it up. Grandma explained that the birds drank the water and they also bathed in it. I thought it was funny that birds had baths and then drank the same water. I did try a taste of my bath water it wasn't very nice as it was soapy. The next time I saw Grandma I told her that I had tasted my bath water and asked why the birds couldn't have a separate container for their drinking water and bath so that the water would taste nicer for them to drink, Grandma just laughed and said birds were different and they didn't mind. After a few years Grandma and Grandad Hutchinson moved from their house onto a new development of bungalows for the elderly, there was a warden who lived in a house on the development. Visiting relatives could stay in a spare room at the warden's house if it was available as the bungalows only had one bedroom. Grandma's health had deteriorated so that is why they moved, she was only a tiny lady and suffered terribly from arthritis which is probably one of the reasons why she was so tiny, her bones had begun to crumble. Grandma's arthritis meant that she couldn't do housework very much. So, Mum would clean the bungalow for them every week. Arthritis is an awful crippling condition and Grandma eventually had to have her toes amputated. I thought that this was wonderful to have a Grandma who was going to have her toes amputated and told everyone at school about it. At that age I had no understanding about how painful and debilitating arthritis was or the pain Grandma was in. I asked her loads of questions about it, Mum said that I shouldn't be asking her, but Grandma didn't mind at all I thought it was great that her feet would be smaller, she laughed and said to me that she might be able to borrow my nice shoes. Grandma had been told that she wouldn't be able to walk afterwards but such was her determination she did walk again, using a walking frame she would shuffle along. Of course, I was fascinated and asked to see her feet without her toes. She showed me them of course and I put her slippers back on for her but was relieved that my nice shoes were too small for her.

Although I had always visited Grandma and Grandad, from about the age of seven I helped Mum clean for Grandma and Grandad when we visited them. I especially loved cleaning the bath and sink, Mum always washed the toilet though, she wanted to make sure that it was done properly. I used to love to 'clean' the bathroom, I would play with all the things in there for ages, I learnt all about floating and sinking in that bathroom, the soap dish floated as did the nail brush, but the soap didn't, Grandads false teeth container certainly floated if it was empty but not as well if it had the solution in it. I wonder if Grandad ever realised that I had emptied the solution out and refilled it with water. He never said anything. Mum eventually used to shout 'Iris, have you finished in there yet?' So, I had to tidy it all up quickly ready for my next job. My other job was cleaning the terracotta tiles in the small covered seating area at the back of the bungalow. First, I had to sweep it clean as leaves and cut grass tended to be collect inside there as they were blown around in the wind, after checking it Mum would give me a bucket of hot water with Izal (a cleaning product) in it, I loved the smell of Izal. I also used lots of vim (that was a white cleaning powder), I would scatter it around making patterns then I used a scrubbing brush and the hot water to remove the dirt left by the leaves and dirt then I used a floor cloth to rinse it all off. It took ages to get rid of all the vim with the floor cloth. I soon learned how to use the vim more sparingly to make the patterns and then it didn't take as much effort to get rid of all the vim. Those products as far as I know are no longer on the market if they were Health and Safety would have a field day now if a child was using these kinds of cleaning products even with rubber gloves I might add but Mum had gone into service at the age of fourteen and it was still expected that girls would help to do the cleaning from a very young age in many families.

When Mum made a pot of tea we all always had china cups and saucers at Grandma's, Mum always used a china cup and saucer throughout her life. At home she always had a china cup but the rest of us had ceramic mugs, my Dad and Ronnie had pint pots. They would drink whole pints of tea! The very thought of drinking a pint of the tea they drank makes me balk, it was very strong tea. When I had my own house, Mum brought her own china cup and saucer to keep at my house as I only had ceramic mugs and had no intention of buying china cups and saucers as they were old fashioned. If Grandad was at home he used to dunk his biscuits and would pour his tea out of his cup into his saucer to drink it, he said the tea was too hot and it cooled down quicker in the saucer. I thought this was great and managed to get away with dunking my biscuits but when I asked if I could have my tea in the saucer. I was told a very firm 'no' and Grandma called Grandad a 'dirty pig,' I thought this was hilarious, but Mum told me to stop saying it when we were walking home when I asked is Grandad a dirty pig because he drinks out of his saucer instead of his cup?' She said, 'it isn't nice to call anyone a dirty pig'. She wouldn't explain why Grandma called him a 'dirty pig' or say anything when I said, 'Grandma isn't nice calling Grandad a dirty pig then'. Poor man I thought he was lovely although I think he had been a disciplinarian with his own kids but that is Grandparents isn't it? You allow your grandchildren to get away with things that your own children wouldn't have been allowed to get away with, but you don't discover that until you become a grandparent.

My Dad's Dad; Grandad Holbrey lived across the road from us My Grandma Holbrey had sadly passed away suddenly just before I moved in to live with my Mum,

Dad and Ronnie. She had known about me and was looking forward to my arrival my Mum and cousins told me this. My Mum used to make Grandad Holbrey a hot meal every day and take it across to him on a plate that she covered with a cone shaped metal cover that had a small maroon handle on it. As I got a little older I could help Grandad Holbrey by going to the Coop shop to do little bits of shopping for him. I thought that I was really grown up and very important. I had to cross two busy roads, I had a list with the money inside and had to make sure that his divvi number was recorded by the shop assistant. I used to take my friends into my Grandad Holbrey's back garden to play I thought it was so nice having a Grandad living so close especially with a huge back garden even though we had a large back garden, being in Grandad's garden meant we were playing out away from our Mums supervision also Grandad used to watch the television or listen to the radio most of the day and he didn't mind us being in his garden. He was a lovely man, my Dad and his brothers resembled him closely in looks and physically. I missed him when he passed away and being able to play in his garden as another family moved into his house.

In my new home, I had my own bedroom, it was a big room we had three double bedrooms. Ronnie's and my bedrooms faced onto the back garden and Mum and Dads faced onto the front garden and the road. There was a blocked off fireplace in my room and there was a photo of Ronnie as a small child in a pedal car on there and I eventually put some things on there too. I had a single bed that was covered with a white counterpane that had large pink flowers and leaves in the centre and in the winter striped flannelette sheets that were very warm to snuggle into. I had heavyweight curtains in the winter and lighter ones in the summer and cotton sheets. There was a wooden wardrobe and a chest of drawers all well polished where all my clothes were neatly hung or folded. There was a patterned carpet in the middle of the room and lino around the outside of the room that was what it was like then, no fitted carpets. Strips of lino were cut to size and slotted under the skirting board and underneath the carpet for a few inches. The lino was washed and polished once a week and the furniture was also polished with beeswax polish. The room had been prepared for my arrival. It was clean bright and nicely decorated for a small child, the wallpaper was lovely it had colourful nursery rhyme pictures with the words printed underneath each picture. I think it was due to these nursery rhymes that I learnt to read so young. Mum and I would sing all the nursery rhymes frequently. Ronnie's room was a proper boy's room with model airplanes hanging from the ceiling and a wooden yacht on display. Mum and Dads bedroom was larger than our bedrooms, there was also a door to a small storage room where the Christmas Tree, suitcases and other things were stored. This tiny room had a small round window in it. On the dressing table there was a hair set, matching brush comb and mirror. There were also some ornaments on there and a container that had talcum powder and a puff to dab it on with.

At the bottom of the stairs was the front door, there were coat pegs on the wall and the door into the living room was opposite the coat pegs. I struggled to hang my own coat up until I worked out that I could reach if

I stood on the third stair and leant over. In the living room there was a coal fire with a built-in oven and hob, you can see these in museums now, we had a gas cooker in the kitchen but there was something nicer about having jacket potatoes and rice pudding cooked in the coal fired oven. Dad's dinner was always kept warm in there ready for when he walked through the door. Before we were going to get North Sea Gas, Mrs Bratby was sat at the table in our kitchen drinking tea and she and Mum were talking about the North Sea Gas and Mrs Bratby was sure that sea water would come out of the gas cooker. I had visions of water spurting from the hobs and through the oven door. In the living room to the left of the fire there was an alcove that had a floor to ceiling cupboard built in, this was divided into two cupboards. The cupboard at the bottom was where I kept my toys and games and the top cupboard which had glass windows was where my tin of matching ribbons were kept and items belonging to Mum and Dad. The alcove at the other side of the fireplace was where the television sat and a small stool that Ronnie had made at school. I loved to sit on that stool watching the tv or colouring at the coffee table. There was a folded wooden dining table that only came out on special occasions and a sideboard where all the best crockery and glasses were stored. There was a door to the pantry this had shelves filled with tins of food. All sorts of things were stored in there including the ironing board and the vacuum cleaner. There was a window that had translucent glass in it that looked out onto the gennel. The small window sill was very useful when my friends and I played in there.

In the kitchen there was a Formica table where we ate all our meals and Mum baked. A cabinet containing the everyday crockery and cutlery. There was a door at one side of the kitchen that led to the bathroom which had a sink and bath. There was another door at the other side of the kitchen that led into a passage which Uncle Charlie (who worked for the council) fitted an outside door to enclose the passage so that it would be warmer. There were two doors leading off the passage one into the toilet. We still needed a paraffin lamp lit in there during the winter to hopefully prevent the water pipes in there from freezing. I can still remember the smell of paraffin and the nice glow the lit lamp gave in the smallest room in the house it was quite comforting having a nice glow in that room! There was also a door into what was supposed to be a coal house, but this was used to store the washing machine, Ronnie's bike, my larger toys and other items such as ladders. The coal was stored outside in a big heap and large pieces of carpet covered it to keep it dry. I often got told off for climbing on top of the coal, there would be a load tapping noise on the kitchen window and Mum's voice shouting 'Iris. Get off that coal now, your socks and knickers will be black, I will never get them clean'. This was serious stuff as it took ages to scrub things clean by hand, now we would just spray stain remover on them or put a special cleaning agent in with the wash in our automatic washing machines.

For me I was living in luxury. For the first time in my life I had a lovely clean home, my own bedroom, toys, books, clothes and I was being nurtured and well cared for and was part of a lovely extended family and community. Prior to living in Oakwood Grange, I had lived with my siblings and birth parents in a small terraced house where they rented one bedroom they only had one double bed until just before I was born when they obtained a single bed that May slept in. May had been horrified at this knowledge when we first discovered this fact as it meant she may have been in the matrimonial bed when I was conceived, I found this hilarious and said, 'I told you that you had always been there for me' after she had said 'but that means that I was there when they, ooh no, horrible'. The house is still standing, I visited it recently. There will be further information about this part of my life later.

Chapter Three

My Childhood Continues

My Dad, as were many men in Maltby and living in the surrounding area was a miner, he was a coalface worker. If he was on days (6am until 2pm), he would come home mid-afternoon so if I wasn't at school I used to wait by the front room window and look down the road for him appearing, when he did appear I used to jump up and down and shout, 'he's coming, he's coming' and Mum would allow me to run down the hill to meet him. He often mentioned later in life about me running down the hill all smiles to greet him and how much it meant to him, during my teens it was an embarrassment of course when he retold these events. I found it fascinating that he and the other miners looked as though they had eye makeup on. Miners still often had what looked like eyeliner on their eyelids even though they had all had showers or baths before coming home. He also had what looked like blue marks under his skin, they were from the coal if they caught their skin on the coal it would remain under their skin. His work clothes that Mum washed consisted of a vest, underpants and thick woollen socks. They were never anything but grey, even Dolly Blue couldn't make them white again due to the coal dust. The woollen socks were darned when they got holes in. He had a helmet, boots and overalls at the colliery, but they remained there in his locker along with the tag number that identified him. Miners took a tag with a number on it before they went down to the coal face and hung it back up on their return to the surface that was the way they knew they were all safely returned to the surface.

Once when Dad was ill in bed, he had been injured down the pit, the Doctor came to visit him. I had received a nurse's set for Christmas, a red vanity case containing all that I needed to be a nurse a little blue dress, a white apron and a white hat with a red cross on it a toy thermometer, bowls and spoons and so the when I knew that the Doctor was coming I put on my outfit ready for his arrival. Dr Hallinen was quite amused and encouraged me to help me. He talked to my Dad, got him to sit up, listened to his chest checked him over and talked some more. After Doctor Hallinen had left I saw myself as his officially appointed nurse and of course I wanted to keep going into bedroom to look after Daddy and make him better. I don't think he appreciated this very much as I continuously climbed onto the bed to get to my patient, he was in pain and needed to rest. I was made to come out of his room and Mum continuously tried to distract me, but I think she was also amused but must have got fed up of me pestering her about needing to go and check if my patient was okay. My chosen career path never included being a nurse.

My Dad nicknamed me rabbit, I think it was because I had been quite timid initially when I went to live with them. I didn't manage to get him to stop calling me this until I was in my teens and he seemed quite upset at this request. When I think back I recall being shy occasionally and wary of strangers but was a very happy child singing, skipping, jumping and running backwards and forwards when I was walking with Mum to visit different family members or going to the shops. Through a child's eyes I could not fault my Dad at all, he would promise me all kinds of things for the future. He occasionally used to take me out for walks with his friends and their children. If we went down through the woods or down the crags the Dads would tell the children the names of the different plants, trees and birds. They taught us how to make noises using pieces of grass between our hands and even whistle, my Mum never appreciated my efforts at whistling like Dad did, I think he tolerated that kind of thing more as he didn't have to put up with it continuously unlike Mum but that is what most Mums did looked after the children full time or definitely for longer periods than the Dads did. One of my memories is of when Dad took me to the cricket field when Freddie Trueman, a famous cricket player of the time, came to Maltby and was playing for some reason, it may have been a fund raiser. Freddie was from Maltby and his Mum still lived there, she went to the hairdressers on Morrell Street every Friday where my Mum also went. If I was on school holidays, I used to help the hairdresser by passing her the rollers and listen to the local gossip, much of which went over my head. I remember frequently being told 'you shouldn't be listening to this' I didn't dare say 'don't say it then'. Dad was not impressed with me at the cricket match when I began screaming loudly. A ladybird had landed on the front of my dress I was terrified that it was going to bite me. It is very funny now, but not at the time, I was given a quick education on insects landing on you and what to do. I still don't like flying insects or birds flying about for that matter. Another bottle of fizzy pop with a straw in and a bag of crisps sorted the problem out and I stopped being upset. These walks and the cricket match with Dad were obviously in the summer as it was always nice weather. It was lovely going out with him, very special times for a small girl and lovely childhood memories that have remained with me. Going back to the hairdressers the lady who owned the business Joan and a younger hairdresser Gail took me to see Father Christmas in Sheffield the first year that I lived with Mum, Dad and Ronnie. Neither Joan or Gail had children, Gail was too young and Joan and her husband an ex RAF pilot had never had children, so I think they not only wanted to give me a treat they wanted to get into the Christmas spirit too. We lined up and went on a little train in the shop to see Father Christmas, the shop was massive, and the shelves were packed with all kinds of colourful items. Christmas music was playing and when I got to see Father Christmas it was magical. He gave me a parcel and in it was a small baking set, a board, rolling pin and cutters. Ideal present for me when I was 'helping' Mum bake. When I got older my Dad used the board to attach the Christmas tree to it so that it wouldn't keep falling over. The Christmas Tree was about three-foot-high and had red berries on it. I was always excited when the tree was decorated and was very proud my board was used.

Mum never smacked me, and I was only smacked by my Dad twice. The first time was when on one day I was dancing around the living room and kitchen singing

'Venus in bloody' instead of 'Venus in blue jeans' Dad was eating his dinner, but he got up from the table and smacked my leg and said don't you ever say that again. I hadn't a clue that 'bloody' was a swear word so at the time I wasn't sure which part I shouldn't say again, was it Venus? All the children at school were singing this song in the playground as a version of a song from a television programme, Fireball XL5. The second time he smacked me was when I and a friend, Jaqueline Thornhill went to another friend's house Bernadette Lewis. Her house was a long way from where we said we were going to be playing, we were not supposed to go off from where we lived but we did, and we had crossed two main roads. When it began to get dark Mrs Lewis asked if we should be going home she had also asked us when we had arrived at her house if our Mums knew we were there, we had said yes knowing full well they didn't. My Mum found us and we both got smacked, me by my Dad when he got in from searching for me. I never did it again and after that my Dad only had to look at me if I was stepping out of line and I stopped whatever I was doing. Although Mum never smacked me I did get told off now and again for being cheeky even in my forties she would say 'you're not too big to get a clip you know' my response as an adult was 'you have to catch me first and it will hurt your hand more than me' as she had arthritis as her mother had before her or 'old Arthur' as she called it.

After that incident of wandering off, I always played on Dunns Dale with the children of my age range until I was older and was aware of the time and the need to get back before Mum realised that I wasn't on the street.

We played most of the time in what was called the circle if there was a big group of us, it was a crossroads where two short roads met Dunns Dale the road had been made into a large circle with the pavements following the circle. It was a great place to play. We played all kinds of games together, one game Tin Can Alley, a form of hide and seek where a tin can is kicked up the road and the person who is on runs off to retrieve it while all the other children run off and hide. If you are caught you must run back and touch the can before the person who is on touches it, otherwise you are on. We also played Hopscotch, what time is it Mr Wolf, the Wolf turns around as the other children walk towards them saying what time it is Mr Wolf? If the Wolf turns around and shouts twelve o'clock the children scatter and try and get back to base otherwise the Wolf catches them to eat for his dinner, it means they become the Wolf. We also played Hot Rice, this is when a small ball is thrown at your legs and if it hits you then you are on, some of the boys threw the ball hard and it would mark your leg if it hit you. We also played marbles, but I didn't like playing for keeps as I wanted to keep all my marbles, and Cowboy and Indians which I didn't like as the boys always wanted the girls to be Indians, they thought because they had toy guns it was their prerogative and sometimes there was only one girl, me. One of the boys, Stephen Matthews would take us into his Grandma's garden to play and as she had rhubarb that was another attraction, Mrs Matthews was lovely and would let us have some of her rhubarb and would make little cone bags out of paper and give us all some sugar to dip the rhubarb in. His Dad had a shed and he used to go fishing and when he had been fishing he showed us some eels, yuk. I may have played mainly with boys, but no way was I touching those slimy things and he also said that they had sharp teeth. My Mum always thought I would marry Stephen. He was a very nice boy but a year younger than me and when you are young a year is a massive age gap, we kissed but never dated we were always with the other children, so I think that was a non-starter, he was a very good-looking lad though. The other children including those younger than me could stay out later than me so when I heard my Mum shout me, from our back door I might add, I would hide behind a wall, she would then walk up the street to find me. I am sure the others pointed to her to tell her where I was, snitches. She knew I was obviously hiding from her but didn't really tell me off I don't know why she didn't just save her voice and come up the street to find me. When I had got ready for bed and was even in my room some of the children were still playing out especially if was the summer as it didn't get dark until late, life seemed so unfair, I used to open my bedroom window to see if I could see them, but the other houses were in the way, but I could still hear them all. The other children could play down in the woods, I wasn't allowed to go down to the woods but did sneak off as I got older and had worked out how to get back to Dunns Dale without my Mum knowing that I had been down there. Mum wanted me to play with a girl who lived on Dunns Dale called Catherine, but I didn't like playing with her, she always bossed me about as she was a bit older. I used to walk to school with Catherine and her Mum for a while. On one occasion, after I had received a blackboard and easel for my birthday she desperately wanted to play with it. Catherine came around to my house to ask if I wanted to play schools and then persuaded me that it would be better to play at her house and that she would help me carry the blackboard and easel. Off we went to her house and she immediately started bossing me about, she hadn't done that outside my back door as my Mum would have heard her. Then she decided she had had enough so went inside her house and shut the door. I then was left with the problem of getting the blackboard and easel back to my house. I carried the easel home first, when Mum saw me she asked me where the blackboard was I told her what had happened, Mum went and got the blackboard, it was far too big and heavy for me to carry. Mum never encouraged me to play with 'that little madam' again and I didn't in fact I don't think I ever spoke to her again and I never walked to school with her again. I think Mum thought I would be more ladylike playing with a girl rather than the boys. Another girl moved into the house next door but one to us, the other side of Mrs Scholey's. Her name was Joan Cartlidge she was a nice girl I think she was a year older, but she never bossed me about. We spent many hours searching the hedges for caterpillars we found some black hairy ones and got a jar put holes in the lid and then put leaves in the jar and the caterpillars. The intention was to keep them so that we could release them when they turned into butterflies. We were told that was cruel and they needed to be in the hedges so had to put them back.

Mum was and still is the most hardworking woman I have ever known. She was always the first person up every morning her years in service had trained her well. Everyone still had a coal fire then in Maltby and there wasn't any central heating until the early seventies and yes, we had ice on the inside of the bedroom windows on cold winter mornings. Mum would make the fire and get the house warm so that everyone else got up to a warm living room and kitchen. By the time we got up Mum would have dusted downstairs, no coal dust in our house for very long, if it didn't move it was cleaned every day. Mum had been in service from the age of fourteen and was always very house proud, this could also be irritating for instance as soon as you stood up she would fluff the cushions up or clear your dinner plate away before the cutlery had even been placed onto the plate ready to be cleared away. She would swoop from wherever she was and would have washed the plate and cutlery before you had finished chewing the last mouthful of food. Mum would also have set the table and prepared breakfast before everyone else was up. I think much of this was due to her training from the age of fourteen and probably before when she was growing up. Mum was always busy even in her eighties she couldn't sit still even though she had inherited her mother's arthritis, she would never give in to it. She was either putting the kettle on, washing up, preparing food, washing, ironing, dusting, vacuuming. She did however have to stop baking as her hands could no longer cope with that.

Mum, like most ladies then had set routines, Monday was washday and if it wasn't a good drying day in our house the washing was hung on the wooden clothes horse that Ronnie had made at school to dry around the coal fire. Steam would be rising off the washing as it dried, and you could smell the washing powder all day. The windows were steamed up with the condensation and Mum constantly wiped them with the window leather. The washing was ironed as soon as it was dry enough and either hung on coat hangers or returned to the clothes horse to air and then put away before the end of the day. On Mondays for dinner we always had the leftovers from Sunday as it was an extremely busy day. We had bubble and squeak (the left-over potatoes mixed with cabbage and then fried) and the leftover meat.

Tuesdays was upstairs day and Thursdays was baking day, I liked baking day. I got to lick out the bowl of cake mixture (we don't do this anymore even though its tasty it is no longer advisable due to raw eggs in the mixture). If I was there I always helped by putting jam in the jam tarts, the coconut tarts, the small Bakewell tarts and lemon curd in the lemon tarts, licking the spoon afterwards of course. I also got to put the Bakewell tart mixture on top of the jam and the coconut mixture on top of the jam once Mum had checked that I had put the correct amount of jam in. Mum also bought Viola bun mixes (packets of cake mixtures) so that I could make some buns myself, I cut the pieces of red and green gelatine into small pieces and placed them evenly in the mixture after I had put it into the small bun cases. I was always proud of my efforts. I was being taught how to bake but Mum never taught me how to make a Sunday dinner. Mum also made egg custard, it took me years to get the pastry right, so I could make my own. No-one has ever made egg custards as good as my Mums so there. Fruit pies were also made, we always had a pudding after dinner every day. I used to complain that Ronnie got bigger puddings than me especially when he got a huge tin dish of rice pudding and I only

got a small one about a quarter of the size of his, it
made no difference I still got a smaller one than him.
The rice pudding was always cooked in the coal oven
until the house was modernised and we lost the coal
fired oven for a small fireplace.

Tuesdays was 'upstairs day', that meant everything
upstairs was cleaned and polished. I was given a very
important job from being very young I was told that I
had to 'keep my eye on the time'. I have always found
that expression funny, which eye are you supposed to
use the right one or the left one? Mum always worked
to a tight schedule, she made sure my Dad's dinner was
ready on time for him returning from work whether he
was on day, afternoon or night shift when he walked
into the kitchen a meal was always on the table immediately. Mum would shout downstairs 'Iris, what time
is it?' Initially I used to shout back 'the big hand is on
the 7 and the small hand is on the 11' (or whatever the
numbers were) Mum than used to shout back what the
time was and that is how I learned to tell the time. I was
quite young when I was given my first watch as a
present. All three bedrooms were thoroughly dusted
and polished and windows cleaned. The carpets were
vacuumed and the lino around the edges was washed
and then polished. The skirting boards were also
washed every week. Spiders, if they managed to get into
our house didn't stay long, cobwebs were gone before
completed. No wonder Mum was always so thin she
never stopped cleaning. In the spring it was spring
cleaning, all the winter curtains were taken down and
the summer ones put up. As I got older and arrived
home from school and later work all the items off the

top of my chest of drawers and window sill were on my bed waiting for me to put them back. On Saturday mornings I had to dust my own chest of drawers and window sill and all the contents on them. I spent ages doing it and used to sing as I did it. Mum always sang when she cleaned so I copied but sang more up to date songs. As I got older, about seven years old, I also 'helped' Mum clean other parts of the house and one of the highlights was dusting her bedroom her dressing table was a treasure trove to me. I would get to handle and used Mums posh hair set to neaten my hair, it consisted of a matching mirror, brush and comb and I could look through the small mirror and see the reflection of the back of my hair in the dressing table mirror. Mums lipstick and blush (the only makeup Mum used) were also there, so I had a peep at those and put a little bit on, just to try, the talcum powder with the fluffy thing you dusted the talc on with was lovely but it went all over the dressing table when I had a try with that so I had to get that cleaned up quickly before mum saw, I am sure she knew what I had been doing as she must have smelled the talcum powder it had a really strong flowery perfume, but she never said anything. I also had access to her jewellery. Mum didn't have expensive jewellery of course but to me it was treasure and I could play with it if I was careful. I think I spent more time playing with Mums things than cleaning. Mum never complained but she far too busy rushing around doing other jobs and it probably prevented me from pestering her. Our house was pristine due to Mums constant cleaning. When I got older I told her I would put a duster in her coffin, so she could keep it clean and be ready when she got to Heaven. I also used to love to stand looking out of Mum and Dads bedroom window it was a much better view from the upstairs window than the living room window. I could see all the comings and goings up and down the street and would tell Mum what was happening. Then she would tell me not to be nosey, that was quite funny as she and her friends and my Aunties appeared to know everyone's business and used to gossip about the latest news bulletins from all over the local area and beyond.

As I have said Mum had been put into service at the age of fourteen that is where she was fully trained in house-work and cooking beyond what she had learned from Grandma. When I got older Mum told me about it. Her Mum took her on the tram to this big house, when they arrived Grandma had a cup of tea with the cook and then left leaving my Mum there. Mum had never met them before. Mum was the housemaid so had to get up early, make the fires and clean the main rooms before the lady of the house got up. Mum also helped the cook by washing up, preparing vegetables and other chores, the cook was nice to Mum (unlike the lady of the house) and became a mother figure to her. Working class people such as Mums family did not have telephones then, so Mum had never answered the phone, now she was expected to and was shown what to do. One day when the telephone rang Mum ran up the steps to answer it but when she had almost reached it she fainted and knocked the phone off its stand. The lady of the house shouted at Mum calling her a 'stupid girl, that could have been something important'. The cook looked after Mum and explained what was happening, Mum had started her first period and had fainted. My

Grandma had not told Mum a thing about periods or anything else about her body. The only thing Grandma told her when Mum went into service was 'don't lie, don't steal and cover up your tuppence'. Mum told everyone that story all her life and of course shared the advice about 'not lying, stealing and covering your tuppence'. Covering your tuppence meant to cover your vagina, do not have sex with boys otherwise you could get pregnant.' No wonder you hear about so many young girls in those days getting pregnant and then being made out to be immoral. They didn't understand what they were doing with the opposite sex could lead to pregnancy. There were quite a few girls that were in service that ended up getting pregnant to the sons of the family they were working for and then lost their jobs. One day the lady of the house asked Mum if she would like to go to a dance. Mum was excited at that prospect and said yes. She was to wear her uniform to go to the dance. The reason for this was so that the Lady of the house could show off to her friends that she had a maid, Mum never got to dance all she had to do was be at the back and call of this vile woman. Mums sister encouraged Mum to leave that place and she went to work in The Rising Sun in Leeds but wasn't old enough to serve in the pub but did other work instead and was happier. When World War Two broke out Mum returned to Maltby as she wanted to work in the munitions factory, but she got into a whole load of trouble as you were not supposed to change jobs during war time according to the people in charge of employment without gaining permission first. Mum was informed if she did it again she could be jailed. She was terrified and went to work in a factory and remained there throughout the war.

Mum was always very caring and made sure she did everything she could to care for me in all ways. However, on one occasion I was not impressed with her at all it was another terrifying incident that I can remember. Mum took me to the clinic before I started full time school. I had to have a preschool check and an injection, that even happens now. I had of course had a previous experience of having an injection at Oakwood Grange Children's Home of course but Mum had not been present during my previous experience. She got the shock of her life as I changed from being the quiet little girl into a screaming banshee lashing out at them all. The traumatic experience of injections in Oakwood Grange was still there I had the injection, but it took them ages and two adults to keep me still so the Doctor could give me the injection. I got a lolly afterwards and a cuddle from Mum. Even though it wasn't a good experience it was better than my previous one and a learning curve for Mum in future when I had to have injections. She did tell everyone for years afterwards what had happened which when I got older was embarrassing and I would remind her that it was cruel making me have injections when I didn't like them.

Mum had to take me to see the GP, Dr Hallinen, for annual check-ups to make sure that I was being looked after properly and thriving due to me being a foster child and on occasions he would 'pop' in to see me at home as he would have to contribute a medical report to Social Services. I liked seeing this Doctor most of the time even though he had a deep voice, he didn't give me injections and always gave me a barley sugar if I went to his surgery. As a small child I used to get a lot of ear infections and tonsillitis, so I didn't like it very much when he said that if I got tonsillitis again I would have to have my tonsils out, I think that would have taken more than two people to pin me down. I did not want to go into hospital and have an operation and injections. Fortunately, I never had to have them removed. Mum looked after me well as a Mum should, she would be up in the night with me if I was ill. I do remember screaming and crying with earache. It is one of the most painful things to have, one of my children suffered from it too. Mum would give me some warm cotton wool and put drops in my ears. I didn't like the medicine she had to give me though. Antibiotics then were foul tasting, they didn't put flavouring in them like they do now to make them more palatable. She would let me lie on the settee during the day with a blanket over me when I was poorly as it was warm in the living room with the coal fire. Mum was also brilliant on Sunday nights. My bedtime was always 8pm but a little Italian mouse puppet called Topo Gigio made an appearance on Sunday Night at the Palladium, I adored Topo Gigio. I was put to bed on time, but Mum would promise to wake me up when Topo Gigio came on and she did. Mum would come upstairs and wake me up and I would go back downstairs and watch Topo Gigio and then would happily go back to bed after this treat.

As most parents will understand going to bed at night can be very time consuming. This was no different for Mum as I had thirteen different dolls and teddies in my bed with me and they all had to be in the correct order to the right and left of me. Then we had a ritual of

MY LIFE MY STORY

saying 'Goodnight God bless, see you in the morning to all the teddies and dolls' and then Mum would tuck me in, kiss me goodnight but as Mum left my bedroom leaving the door slightly open and make her way downstairs I would keep shouting 'Mummy' she would reply 'yes' and then I would repeat the whole 'Goodnight, God bless, see you in the morning' process again. She never appeared to get cross, but she must have been to the point of exasperation after repeating the whole process about half a dozen times! I wasn't frightened about going to bed at all I just liked to keep Mum for longer at the end of the day. My Dad never put me to bed that I can recall.

Mum taught me how to skip and play two balls against the wall teaching me the rhymes that she had learnt as a girl. She also taught me how to knit and hand sew, I would spend hours making clothes for my dolls using my new-found skills. When any of us had new shoes then I would use the shoe box and make a bed for one of my dolls. I would cut up old pillowcases that Mum gave me and make them into mattresses and bedding. I was given a piece of net curtain once and so my doll had a posh bed. It was a four-poster bed made from a shoe box complete with lace curtains. If my Mum was darning my Dads pit socks, then I would be sewing my dolls new clothes. By doing all these activities together Mum was constantly communicating with me and teaching me how to communicate with other people in a polite manner. We had a very close relationship due to the time she spent with me and the care that she gave me throughout my childhood and adulthood.

I have always loved doing crafts and loved to draw pictures and colour abstract patterns and gave some of these to Miss Short my social worker. She stuck them up in her office. Miss Short provided me with wool to knit clothes for my dolls. When I received a painting by numbers set with oil paints I thought I was a real artist. Later, I discovered that two of my birth siblings were very talented at drawing, but I have never been able to draw, or sketch animals or people like them.

Mum would look at books with me and listen to me read and think it is due to her attention and the interest that she paid me that I could read and write so early in my life. I was almost like an only child as Ronnie was much older than me and when he was living at home he was out with his friends most of the time. So, I got lots of attention from my Mum. I attended a nursery just down the road from our house, on Walters Road before I started full time school. It was a one storey prefab building it had a small play area and some grass to play on. Next door was an identical building that was the clinic. I can remember waking up from the nap, all the children still had a nap after dinner, when I opened my eyes I saw two of the ladies that looked after us they were talking to each other in very quiet voices and one of the ladies was writing on the board, I shouted across to her 'that says chicken' she turned around and looked amazed. Then I was told to be quiet as the other children were still asleep, but I heard them say 'how on earth can she read that?' After the children had all woken up we had milk and biscuits but nothing else was said about me reading the word on the board. My Dad had the Daily Mirror delivered and I used to grab it and read it as soon as it came through the door at this age too, I think I was copying my Dad reading the paper. I loved the cartoon Andy Capp and would find that page first. I laughed when his wife Flo was pictured being cross with him and was pictured waving a rolling pin at him and when Flo plonked Andy's dinner on the bar in the pub in front of him I laughed so much it was hilarious to me taking his dinner to the pub. I would of course share the cartoon with my Mum and she would laugh. If my Dad was in he used to ask me if he could have his newspaper and I used to say, 'I haven't finished yet'. I am amazed I didn't get told off for that, he then used to ask me for the back pages I gave him them as I wasn't interested in the sports pages. Dad liked to bet on the horses, so he wanted to read those pages. Mum used to tell me off frequently about my reading as I used to be so engrossed in a book that I genuinely hadn't heard her call me numerous times to come to the table for dinner. I loved sitting at the table for my meals but before I sat down I always checked it was my stool, I had written my name under one of the stools as soon as I could write my name, there were two chairs and two stools it was important that I sat on my own stool, I think that I was marking out my territory. Mum must have seen it as she cleaned everything, but she never said anything about me writing my name under the stool.

Ronnie was at home initially, when I went to live with them he was fourteen. I remember him going to school he made some items in woodwork, I especially liked sitting on the little stool that he had made. I adored Ronnie, I loved having a big brother and he was very patient with me when I pestered him well I think he was

I probably ignored the signals if he wasn't. I remember my Dad trying to help him with some maths homework on one occasion it sounded very complicated and I don't think Dad was a lot of help as he said, 'it's different to how we did maths'. Ronnie joined the army for a short time after leaving school, so I ended up almost being an only child for a while. I loved it when Ronnie came home on leave and would pester my Mum constantly asking which day he was coming back, what time would he arrive home. On the day he was coming home I would be constantly at the front room window looking down the street, I would get told off for making marks on the window if I wiped it with my hand or my sleeve if it had steamed up. I used to help Mum keep Ronnie's room clean and tidy but was not allowed to dust his model airplanes. Mum used to get told off for breaking bits off them, but she still dusted them, I think she thought that Ronnie wouldn't notice if the odd propeller or other bits were missing. Ronnie left the army and returned home, we were a family of four again. I went to school and Ronnie went to work. Ronnie had a double bed in his room, I didn't mind that at all and when his girlfriend Sheila stayed over I slept in his bed with her and I snuggled right up to her, Ronnie slept in my room in my single bed. Unmarried couples didn't sleep together in their parent's homes then. I think Ronnie would call it tormenting but I loved Sheila to bits and would chatter away to her and keep her fully informed about everything that had happened since I had seen her the last time, he didn't get away with a thing. Mum was also kept fully informed by me, if they were kissing, I would run into the kitchen and say 'Mum, Mum they are kissing!' she would tell me to leave them alone, I did for a few minutes. If I got the chance I would run into my room and wake Ronnie up in the morning if Sheila was staying over, I even discovered he was naked on one occasion, so Sheila was duly informed. She didn't do what I asked though when I said, 'come and see'. I hope Mum changed my bed after he had slept in it!

Sheila was brilliant with me and spent a lot of time with me. Ronnie and Sheila bought me a doll with long blonde hair and a green velvet dress as a present once. Sheila even took me swimming to the outdoor pool in Maltby to teach me to swim I thought that was fabulous, Sheila was the first grown up that I saw naked. Afterwards I asked Mum loads of questions, I wanted to know if I would have a lady's body like Sheila and when would it happen, but Mum never answered my questions, she avoided them saying things like 'you will have to wait and see'. Wait and see, I wanted to know all about getting bigger and what it felt like to have breasts and hair where I didn't have any now. I frequently looked to see if things were changing and took note of my female cousins.

Mum was always embarrassed about the body and its functions, so I remained confused about quite a few things especially how babies got in and out of lady's tummies. That question was asked by me a great deal as my Mum and Aunties topic of gossip was often about who was having a baby and when it was due. Another confusing thing was when we went to the supermarket Mum used to buy some things that were quickly put into a plain brown paper bag at the till as though no one should see them. I kept asking what they were so Mum said 'a surprise parcel' I thought it was a surprise for me so continually pestered her about it, eventually she said, 'you will find out when you are older'. Very puzzling, I eventually found out they were sanitary towels. Why women used to talk in whispers about women being pregnant I will never be able to fathom out. If the girl was unmarried it was serious and gossiped about a great deal as though they had done something horrendous, no mention about the boy who had got them pregnant though, it was as though there was a different code of conduct for girls and boys. I asked my Mum loads of times 'how does the baby get in the lady's tummy and how does it get out?' I hadn't worked out that the baby didn't go in as anything other than a baby. I thought it must be like putting a fully-grown baby in the lady's tummy for some reason maybe to let it grow bigger like a small plant and then taking it back out again when it was big enough. I eventually found out after May told me when I was about eleven what really happened. John or Ken had told her. Neither May or I were impressed with that at all and we decided we were not going to do that until we got married. There was no way we were going to get pregnant and be gossiped about.

Mum was always very polite and proper. Manners were extremely important to her. So, to be polite I will say that Mum had flatulence on one occasion, she said excuse me, but I burst into fits of giggles as that is what we did at school if anyone did it, she looked at me and said that she had fluffed and that even the Queen fluffed. That made me giggle even more as I could not imagine the Queen in her crown and ceremonial robes 'fluffing' and I shared my new-found knowledge with everyone, that my Mum fluffed just like the Queen. I wonder what the Queen would make of that? The word fart is used frequently now how times have changed but people still giggle especially children.

In the summer we would have a family holiday, we went to Southport most years and stayed at the same boarding house ran by a Mr and Mrs Green. The same families were there that week every year so we all met up and went to the beach together. The children would all have buckets and spades and played together making sandcastles that we put the colourful little flags that we had bought from the shops near to the beach. One-year Ronnie made this huge boat with seats in the sand, we younger children had a great time playing in it. Ronnie had a big yacht that he could sail on the lake at Southport. As I wanted to be like Ronnie I was bought a small red one and told not to let it go too far from the side as my Dad didn't want to go paddling into the water after it. The ladies would go to a café in the morning and have a cup of tea. Mum didn't have sugar in her tea, so she used to give me the two sugar lumps that were wrapped in paper to save until later to give to the donkeys that gave children rides on the beach. On one holiday to Southport I was taken to see Sooty and Harry Corbett his original owner, it was brilliant, and I had a photograph taken with a life sized Sooty and Harry. I still have the photograph but not the mug or the egg cup I also got. Mum and I went to the cinema one night to see 'Thoroughly Modern Milly' that Julie Andrew played the lead role in I loved it. An incident I remember that upset me was when Mum and Dad went on a speed boat and I had to stand and watch them. I screamed and cried as it scared me as the boat went so fast. The poor man who took the money from the customers tried to reassure me, but I was pleased when they were back on dry land with me. There was a big park in Southport and the gardens were beautiful, so we would always visit there. Even as a child I appreciated the floral displays and especially the huge working clock that had lovely coloured sections made from the different flowers and plants. We also took some bread to feed the ducks.

There was a gong in the hall at Mr and Mrs Greens boarding house that was hit to inform all the guests that it was meal time. All the children would excitedly line up before meal times as the gong was hit, and we took it in turns to bang the gong over the week, Mr Green oversaw the gong and made sure that we all had at least one turn during the week. We all ate in our family units at the table that had been allocated to us for the week. After dinner in the evening the children and the Dads would often go into the back garden, the children to play and the Dads to have a cigarette and chat. It was lovely seeing everyone every year. It was like being in a large extended family. Mum and the other ladies would write to each other during the year to keep up to date with family news and plan for the following holiday or visits to each other's houses.

We stayed in Manchester once at one of the family's homes who used to go to Southport at the same time as us, the house was near the Kellogg's factory. Whilst we were staying there we spent a day in a huge park, we travelled there on a small train. In the park were deer and other animals. There was also a fairground visiting a park near to their house we visited that, and we had a go at winning things on hook a duck, my Dad won a ceramic tea caddy on the shooting range. I was so proud of him winning something so nice.

One year we visited my Mums brother, Uncle Joe in Liverpool but we stayed with his ex-wife, Auntie May and their daughter Pat as Uncle Joe only lived in a one bedroomed flat. Pat and her friends used to be listening to all the same 1960's music as Ronnie and my other cousins in Maltby did. The Beatles were very popular then and I would sing along. Uncle Joe was Mums oldest brother, in his living room he had tropical fish in huge tanks (well they seemed huge to me). They were amazing, and I was fascinated with the beauty and the colours of them and how the different types of fish swam differently. When Uncle Joe was showing me the baby fish being born and how he needed to move them out of the tank to safety, so they wouldn't be eaten by the other fish, my Mum told him off for letting me see the fish being born. My Dad said it was fine but Mum said it wasn't right I shouldn't be seeing such things. Uncle Joe and Dad just smiled at each other I was totally absorbed in the wonder of it all and hoping that Uncle Joe could rescue all the baby fish, he was my hero for saving the babies. On one of the days we went on the ferry across the Mersey to New Brighton. As we were docking Dad pointed out to me the jellyfish around the ferry, he told me how you should never stand on one if they have been washed up on the beach as they will sting you, to me my Dad was the font of all knowledge he was the cleverest person I knew. There was a small fairground and Dad won me a little brooch on the fair, it was one of my treasures that like many disappeared over the years. We, or rather I spent ages watching the Punch and Judy show I thought it was brilliant especially when the dog ran off with the sausages and when Judy hit Punch it reminded me of Andy Cap and Flo a cartoon in my Dad's paper the Daily Mirror. Mum and Dad sat on a wall keeping an eye on me. Once our holiday ended we caught the train from Lime Street Station to go home. The carriages were like those found on the Steam Train lines now with separate compartments with two rows of three seats facing each other and a door into the corridor. On the way back on the train from Liverpool to Sheffield I was put outside the carriage into the corridor as I had continuously from leaving Lime Street sang the Beatles popular hits especially 'She loves you yeah' over and over again, the adults didn't appreciate my singing skills, or they didn't like the Beatles. So, after a few warnings from my Dad into the corridor I went. I continued singing in the corridor and no one that passed me complained, I was also happier in the corridor anyway as I could also dance around.

In the summer Mum and I, as many other families in Maltby and across the country did, went to the coast on day trips with the different workings men's clubs that Dad was a member of. These trips were during the week, so Dad and Ronnie were both at work for most them. We all went on coaches, there was a coach firm in Maltby, but they didn't have enough coaches for the number of people going so coaches from the surrounding area were hired. It was even more exciting when it was one of the trips for the club on Walters Road just around the corner from where we lived as the adult coaches parked up on our road and the children's coaches, (the children went on different coaches to the adults) were parked on Walters Road outside The Slip as the club was called locally. I would be bouncing up and down hopping from one foot to the other with excitement shouting can we go and get on the coach yet? Mum was still tidying up and making a picnic for herself after breakfast. I was really worried they would go without us when we wouldn't be leaving for at least half an hour. I think the other coach trips were a little easier for Mum as I couldn't see the coaches arrive. It was if I saw any coaches driving down the main road towards the British Legion then I would start to get excited and try and get Mum to walk even faster than she always did. The Dads would pay in so much a week to fund these trips and for the extra things for the children. The children all wore an identification label tied with string so if they got lost they could be easily returned to where they should be, they had the child's name, club name and coach details on them. When we arrived at Cleethorpes or Mablethorpe, which were always the destinations, before our parents came to collect us off the bus we were on, the children were each given a paper bag that contained a packed lunch, a small brown envelope that contained some tickets for the rides and some spending money. The children were also provided with a fish and chip tea at the end of the day before getting back on their buses to return home. After the parents had collected their offspring from their coaches the different family groups went off for the day together. Most families went straight to the beach and the adults would get deckchairs for themselves and settle all the children down to eat their packed lunches. Of course, as soon as the children were on the beach they played in the sand, so our sandwiches were always gritty from the sand on our hands. The adults would bring their own packed lunches and usually a flask of tea. We all spent a few hours on the beach digging and making sandcastles and sand pies. Most people then visited the funfair, after the children's lunches had settled down was the adults excuse of course. One year I desperately wanted to go on the waltzes, but I didn't have anyone to go on with. My older cousins were all working now so they no longer came on the day trips and neither did their parents. Our next-door neighbour, Mrs Bratby, her daughter Brenda, grandson Paul, my Mum and I spent the day together. Paul was younger than me and he wouldn't be allowed on the ride. My Mum refused go on it with me as did Brenda despite Mrs Bratby saying to them 'come on one of you go on with the poor lass', they still refused to so Mrs Bratby being such a superstar said. 'Here hold my bag, I will go on with the lass, come on'. I am not sure how old she was but to me she appeared to be very old. She had a grandson who was a teenager, so she must have been in her sixties. We got on the ride and pulled the safety bar down and were fine at first as the ride set off slowly and we went around a few times up and down but not spinning around very much. Then one of the lads operating the ride came and spun us around, I loved it and laughed louder and louder the faster we spun around as the ride increased in speed. We both held onto the bar tightly and Mrs Bratby also laughed at first but then she became quiet and didn't look very happy in fact she didn't look very well the colour of her face changed and she passed out. The lad who had spun us was at the other side of the ride by this time spinning someone else around. Mum and Brenda had been standing at the side of the ride watching the whole thing and laughing and waving at us and at first Mrs Bratby had said 'wave to your Mum, there she is look'. Brenda was also laughing and waving and then she was laughing even more because she could see her Mum had slumped down in the seat, her legs were also open, and you could see her big knickers, they were white and came to just above her knees, Brenda and my Mum stopped laughing as they realised that Mrs Bratby had passed out. Brenda and Mum then came up the steps on to the side of the ride and were waving and shouting frantically at the men operating the ride to stop it. The men eventually saw them and stopped the ride, we had been on ages anyway, so I think we had got our money's worth, I certainly had as I loved the car spinning around fast but was worried about Mrs Bratby passing out. When the ride fully stopped Brenda and Mum ran onto the ride to our carriage and Brenda was trying to stop the car from moving from side to side and when she had done that she climbed into the car and tried to get Mrs Bratby to wake up. Brenda asked one of the men to get a cup of water and he ran off and quickly came back with a cup and offered it to Mrs Bratby who promptly threw it onto the lad that had been pushing us round and called him a name. I can't remember the exact word but knew that I hadn't heard it before. Brenda and Mum managed to get Mrs Bratby up onto her feet, she was still very wobbly when walking so they helped her down the steps one at either side of her and sat her on a seat.

It took her ages for Mrs Bratby to stop feeling dizzy. I was getting bored waiting around for Mrs Bratby to stop feeling dizzy so asked if I could go on another ride, the Big Dipper, I didn't get a very positive response to that at all. No stamina some people! Mrs Bratby did talk about her experience on the waltzes for a long time afterwards and would laugh about throwing the water on the young lad who had spun the car. I would have loved to have gone on the Big Dipper that day, but Mum had wet herself when she went on the one in Blackpool when she was younger so no chance of that. Maybe if Mrs Bratby hadn't fainted she would have been game for that too, I like to think so.

From the age of three until nine my life was good I was settled in a nice home and extended family that had accepted me as one of theirs, I was a happy and contented child and felt safe. All the neighbours and a great many people in Maltby knew me as Maltby was a much smaller place than it is now, and my Mum, Dad, Ronnie and other relatives had all grown up there. Mum and I could never walk down the main street without bumping into people that she knew. I had always been told that I had another family somewhere, but it didn't really mean much to me. I don't think small children rationalise things in that way. As far as my understanding went, I had a Mum and Dad and a brother called Ronnie. I had Grandma and Grandad Hutchinson and Grandad Holbrey. I had all my Aunties and Uncles and their children were my cousins. I was just like my school friends and my friends on Dunns Dale. I did sort of understand that May and Irene were my sisters as I had always been told that but thought they lived where they lived and that was it that was normal for May, Irene and I. Our foster parents were excellent in making efforts to keep the three of us in regular contact, but it wasn't ever all three of us together it was May and I or Irene and I. Mum and I visited Irene every Friday at her home in Bramley which wasn't very far away from Maltby, just a short bus ride away. We would get a bus from Maltby and we were there in about 20 minutes. I visited May frequently too although she lived two bus rides away, Mum and I would catch a bus to Rotherham and then catch a bus to Wath upon Dearne so that took us a whole day to visit May. My Dad never learnt to drive but May's Dad had a car and so they used to visit our house too. Irene's Mum and Dad never visited our house or Mays, but they did have other children and their Dad was often at work late, so it was more difficult for her Mum to visit us. As far as I was concerned May lived with her Mum and Dad and had a sister called Linda and a brother called Gary. Irene lived in Bramley and she lived with her Mum and Dad and her sister Ann, Brother Alan, a baby sister called Dawn and later another baby sister, Jane. Irene stayed at my home when her Foster Mum had a baby and I stayed at May's when my Mum had to go into hospital for an operation. I was a bridesmaid with May at her foster sister Linda's wedding. One of my Mum's sisters; Auntie Winnie was a brilliant dressmaker and made all the bridesmaid dresses. They were a pale blue with white daisies sewn on them. We also wore short blue veils on a headdress and white shoes and socks we were given a silver bangle as a present for being bridesmaids. I managed to spill orange pop down my dress at the reception my Mum wasn't very pleased with me about that as she thought that she wouldn't be able to get the stain out of the dress. Although I had always been told they were my sisters it really didn't register fully that we might end up having to leave our Mums and Dads to go to live together with different people that were our birth Mother and Father. It still wasn't like being sisters, we had been raised in different families for seven years. We were robbed of being 'proper' siblings but also, we gained by not being with Jack and Sheila all our lives. I also had two cousins Carol and David who my Mum's sister Doreen and her husband Ben had adopted so I thought that I was like them really, I would stay in Maltby with everyone I knew.

When I visited Irene on a Friday after school if it was nice weather and light we would play outside together. I remember one summer during the harvest going to a field near their house and building a den with the bales of hay alongside a group of her friends and her foster brother Alan. If it was wet or dark outside, then we would play in the house whilst our Mums had a cup of tea and caught up with each other's news about members of the individual families. All three of our Mums knew about each other's families and supported each other in keeping all three of us in contact with each other. This was not organised by our social workers it was due to the kindness of the three ladies who fostered three little girls who were sisters but separated through no fault of their own. They ensured that we at least grew up during our formative years knowing each other.

Our worlds were blown apart when we were told that we were going back to live with our birth parents and brothers. What on earth did that mean? Who were these people? At the age of nine I didn't understand, and Irene was only eight, so I think perhaps she had even less understanding than May and I or maybe was the same. I remember being told by the social worker that it would be exciting living with my brothers and sisters. What a stupid thing to say, we were all settled after 7 years. I didn't even know that I had any other brothers. Interestingly there was no mention of any older sisters at that point in time.

During the time that we had been in care our birth parents had made little effort to see us. The children's office (social workers) would organise parental visits at the Children's Office in Rotherham and our Mum's would take us along to the Children's Office only to find that they hadn't turned up or notified the social workers that they would not be coming to the meetings. They made no effort to arrange any meeting dates with us, they were busy getting on with their own lives and had even relocated to Chesterfield which is in Derbyshire when we all still lived in South Yorkshire. What kind of a parent would move to another county away from their children? Our birth father Jack could also be very aggressive towards the social worker. In fact, on one visit to the children's offices, Jack had frightened us all with the aggressive behaviour he displayed in front of us and our Mums had to calm us down. Our Mums were asked by the social services staff to take us away from the shouting and aggressive behaviour and we were duly taken home. On this and other occasions he was reported for his behaviour to a senior member of social services. So there had been an ongoing history of them not attending pre-arranged visits to the children's offices to see us and to which our Mums had always taken us to. It didn't really mean anything to me as I didn't know who they were anyway I had only seen them twice since I was two years old, but I was frightened of the man who was shouting and being nasty. There was also a history of them not signing and returning papers that were giving permission for us to have things such as vaccinations and for me to attend hospital appointments at the optometry department for my eyes. We never received any birthday cards, Christmas cards, presents or any contributions towards our keep. It was as though we didn't exist to them. Although our foster parents received an allowance it wasn't enough for all our costs and we were given much more from them in material possessions.

My Mum hadn't informed me that the people we were going to live with was the man who had been shouting at the children's offices, I didn't want to go to live with strangers, Irene didn't, and May certainly didn't but if we had known that it was him, the man that shouted that we were going to live with then it would have been even more so. Our lives were with our Mums, Dads and foster siblings in our homes with all our familiar things, going to our school to see our friends, learning how to read, write, and do maths and all the other fun stuff. I was very frightened no matter what they said to me. Then as I could write independently I was even made to write to these people that I didn't know. The Social Worker began to try and build a bond with people I had only seen twice by writing to them. The visits to the children's offices didn't increase. There were no 'supervised' visits for us either that would monitor the interaction between parents and children. As an adult with a great deal of experience of working with children and young people, I think it was ridiculous and not well thought out or managed appropriately at all.

On one visit Mum and I made to May's home in Wath upon Dearne after this devastating news, the adults wanted to talk in private, so we were sent outside. This wasn't unusual though as they always liked to have a chat without us listening. May and I were playing outside behind their garage and we were frantically trying to make a fire by rubbing two sticks together, May had convinced me that we could make a fire and that it would work if we rubbed the sticks together really hard. I don't know what we were going to do if we had managed to make a fire I think we would have been in trouble. Anyway, I went along with it as May was older than me and was quite bossy as most little girls tend to be towards younger ones. Previously I had also believed May when she had told me that you could hypnotise someone by swinging a yoyo in front of their eyes on one visit to my house. On that occasion we were playing in my bedroom when they had come to visit us one evening and May tried to hypnotise her foster brother Gary with my yoyo. Gary was a little older than us but always did what May told him. It didn't work on him and Gary and I were told by May that it was Gary's fault as he wasn't concentrating so May tried again. We gave up on that after several attempts as Gary obviously just wasn't doing it properly, he didn't stare hard enough or long enough at the yoyo. I think he was probably cross eyed by that point.

Anyway, as we were trying to make the fire behind the garage May was telling me that they were definitely going to take us away from our Mums and Dads and they were going to make us live with our 'real' Mother and Father, she informed me that our Mother was a wicked witch. May informed me that she had long black hair that was really scruffy and that she rode a broomstick, was very cruel and hurt children.

Out of the mouths of babes........little did we know what was to come.

Chapter Four

Confusing Times

I was very confused and even more frightened at May's revelation that our birth mother Sheila was a witch. All I knew about witches was that they were very scary, and they did evil spells and had cauldron's and put horrible things like frogs and spiders in the cauldron with weeds and stirred it all together. They also flew on broomsticks like May had said. They were also ugly and had large bent noses and warts on their faces had long dirty nails and long dirty black hair. On several occasions I asked my Mum if it was true. She told me that May is being silly, don't listen to things like that. I still wasn't convinced and was worried and decided that I would have to be very careful.

This business of having to go and live with our 'real mum and dad' wasn't new but by then I had forgotten about the first time it had nearly happened. My Mum informed me that when I was four she had sat me down one day to have a talk with me after a visit from Miss Short, my social worker. She told me that I had to go and live with my 'real' Mum and Dad I don't think at that age I had any understanding of what this meant as at nine I didn't fully understand it. I was bound to be confused at this even though I had always been told that May and Irene were my sisters it hadn't really registered that I could end up having to live with my birth parents and May and Irene, I didn't really understand what 'birth parents' meant. Also, I didn't know my birth parents at all when I was four. Why would I? I hadn't seen them since I was two I had forgotten them. They hadn't visited us or made any contact through birthday cards or Christmas cards. I didn't want to leave my Mum, Dad and Ronnie to go and live somewhere else I wanted to stay at my house, sleep in my bedroom and play with my toys and my friends. Mum tried to reassure me that I would be okay, and that I would be with May and Irene all the time, and that it would be good fun having my sisters to play with all the time. On the day I was to be picked up all my belongings had been packed and ready, so Mum and I waited for Miss Short to arrive, she didn't arrive, but a letter from Miss Short did. The letter informed Mum that I would not be returning to my birth parents that day and Miss Short would call to discuss with Mum in due course. My Mum then had to explain to me that I wasn't going to live with my 'real' Mum and Dad that day. Mum and I unpacked all my things and put them back where they belonged. At least we had been given a reprieve at that point. May, Irene and I continued to live with our Mums and Dads and saw each other regularly. Years later I found out the reason for this decision after I obtained some of my records of being in care and following the death of another birth sister Maggie, her records which gave a better picture of the history of what had happened to us and why.

My home life settled down again and I continued to have a great childhood playing with my friends, visiting Aunties, Uncles, Cousins, Grandad Holbrey, Grandad and Grandma Hutchinson and my Mums friends. Maltby as I have stated was quite a small place when I was growing up. It had a colliery 'Maltby Main', where many of the men had worked for generation after generation and a housing estate had been built to house families that had moved to Maltby to work in the colliery. There were also factories, ones that made tools, one that made boots and shoes and another that made knitwear so many of the other residents of Maltby worked in these factories. Fathers, Mothers, Aunties, Uncles working alongside the younger members of the family and their neighbours. It was as though everyone knew everyone else in some way or another. So, when Mum and I walked down the High Street it took ages as Mum knew so many people and would be asking them about their relatives and they would do the same to her. They would discuss any local news, births, deaths and marriages and any gossip. They would always speak to me as well asking how I was, what school was like, if I had had a good birthday, Christmas, holiday or whatever. Initially I was shy and used to hide behind my Mum, but she would say 'Iris, it's rude not to speak to someone if they say hello to you'. I remember saying 'but I don't want to speak to strangers, you said not to'. I remember some of the ladies laughing and saying I was right. I soon got to know them and would then speak to them first, in fact if Mum was in a hurry she ended up having to say 'sorry, we have to get back otherwise dinner won't be ready in time for Clag (my Dad) getting back from work'. I made even more friends once I started school and would play with them in school and at the park when I was old enough to go there with a group of friends. It was also the same when we visited the different shops. As I got older and was out and about by myself then Mum and Dad's friends would always speak to me and ask if they were okay and ask me about what I was doing. It was a very nice community to live and grow up in.

After leaving the Nursery I went to school. Maltby Crags School was lovely. It was a Victorian building that faced onto countryside; the Crags at one side. In the infant's class I joined the road safety group the Tufty Club. I continued to develop my reading and writing skills and learned about lots of new things. I played in the play house with my classmates, went down the Crags and did nature walks during the afternoon and stuck the plants that I found in my workbook after we returned. The Crags is an area of land, green fields and rocks and paths that you can walk along. When I was in the infants on the day of the Christmas party my friends and I stood at the fence looking onto the Crags and told the dinner ladies that we could hear Father Christmas' sleigh, we had totally convinced ourselves that we had heard him. When I was six we all wrote letters to Father Christmas to tell him what we would like for Christmas. The letter that I had written was read out to the class and the teacher asked us what was good about it. She informed us all that it was because I had used the word 'or' in my letter I hadn't written a long list of things I wanted. She said that Iris won't be disappointed on Christmas morning as she should receive at least one of the things that she has asked for.

We all got a lecture about being selfish then and that toys were expensive. My Mum was bringing me up to share and to not ask for lots of things. My pocket money was managed by me from a very early age and I decided with my Mums advice to save some of it for special occasions. On Monday, Tuesday and Friday I bought myself some sweets on the way to school, I often bought a small tin of Imps, they were tiny liquorish sweets they weren't my favourite sweets I just liked the tins and would use them to save the rest of my pocket money in. For the Christmas party we had all taken some food into school for the party and could wear party dresses instead of the usual gymslips and cardigans, we played games such as pin the tail on the donkey and musical chairs which was always popular with the boys. Christmas was always exciting for me when I was growing up and into adulthood. With my Mum, Dad and maybe Ronnie, I would hang one of my dad's socks on the mantlepiece and it always had fruit and some coins in it on Christmas morning and there was a pillowcase that had presents in at the bottom of my bed too. Christmas mornings were very noisy as soon as I woke up I always received lovely presents and was never disappointed.

When I moved from the infants into the juniors I began learning how to write using a pen and ink and do joined up writing it was great I loved going to school. Playtimes were great too, we played in groups boys with boys and the girls with the girls. I didn't quite understand this as I always played with the boys at home as it was mainly boys on our street and I didn't like the girl who was my age that lived near me as she was far too bossy. My cousin Rebecca who is three months younger than me was in the same class as me, but our other cousins had moved on to secondary school or had left school and were working by the time we were in the junior school. All the Mums knew each other and so they were aware that I was a foster child, but they always treated me the same as any of the other children, I never felt out of place, I was fully integrated into the social life in and outside school. My Mum worked as a dinner lady, preparing the dinners for a while at the Crags School during the time I attended there. I thought that was great and my friends and I used to go and wave to her through the kitchen window at playtimes. That did get me into bother on one day as I took the veil that I had worn as a bridesmaid into school despite my Mum saying that I couldn't when I had asked her if I could take it to show my friends. Mum saw me with the veil on at playtime, so I was called across to the kitchen by her and she took it off me and told me off. When I was going to be leaving the Crags school and Maltby I think my school friends and my friends on Dunns Dale were very confused and maybe more confused than me. I suppose their Mums would have had to explain everything to them. I did see some of them when I went back home for all the school holidays especially if they were playing on Dunns Dale or were on the park, but children grow up, change friends and move on. So even though I went back home during the school holidays it was never the same as it had been. I am glad that I did go back home during the school holidays as life would have been so much worse for me if I hadn't been able to do that.

I should explain that I always refer to my birth parents as Jack and Sheila as they do not in my mind deserve that status of being called my Mum and Dad and I never called them Mummy and Daddy which is what I called my Mum and Dad when I was very young. Anyway, I should explain why May, Irene and I did not return to live with Jack and Sheila on that day when I was four. They did not have suitable accommodation for us to live in. They were in effect homeless and were living in an old single decker bus in a field with two young children, Tommy (his registered name was Tom, but we always called him Tommy and he will always be Tommy to my siblings and I) and a baby, my brother Robert. In the bus there was only one double bed with no bedding, they used coats as blankets There was a pram that the baby slept in and a settee. No bathroom, running water or heating. Who in their right mind would want to or think that they would rather have their nine children living in a bus in a field rather than in the nice warm homes that they were living in? My own thoughts on this are that it surrounds the benefits that they would be able to claim by having that many children living with them. Thankfully Social Services inspected where they were living and of course said no. Some readers would probably feel sorry for them and say that Social Services should have found somewhere for them to live and say that the council should have given them a house. Don't be deluded, you see as I have already stated they had made no effort in seeing us, Jack was not working through his own choice, there were other reasons not to give them a council house other than there being others on the waiting list who were probably more deserving.

Before May, Irene and I were born Jack and Sheila had four children taken off them due to the cruelty and neglect they inflicted on them. The NSPCC, their GP and the local vicar were involved in this child protection issue over a significant amount of time. Jack and Sheila were very fortunate at that time to be living in a brand-new NCB (National Coal Board) house, 55 Zamar Crescent, Thurcroft, South Yorkshire as Jack worked or was supposed to work at Thurcroft Colliery and therefore qualified for a NCB house. He was according to the court records able to earn a very good wage as a coal face worker. Jack however didn't like going to work and so he didn't go. In court he made all kinds of excuses including that 'she (meaning Sheila) spends the day canting with neighbours' (canting means gossiping) and wasn't cleaning the house. How did he know this if he was at work? He wouldn't be able to see what she was doing although the house was very dirty as were the four small children. He was very good at going out and staying out all night with Sheila not knowing where he was or who he was with. At this time Jack was still married to someone else and had a daughter with her. Jack and Sheila didn't marry until Sheila was five months pregnant with their fifth child, May. Due to Jack refusing to go to work they didn't have enough money to feed and clothe the four children or furnish the house. Neither of them liked to look after the house or garden and the house was very dirty, they didn't look after the children either. Sheila would go and beg for food, clothes and money from the Vicar of Thurcroft and anyone else who she thought would listen. Jacks sister, Doris lived close to them at a place called Dinnington and would visit them. Doris informed May and I years later that she hadn't been happy with the situation and travelled from Dinnington to Thurcroft often and cleaned the house and bathed and dressed the children in new clothes. She tried to 'train' Sheila to do the same as she did. After visiting on several occasions and seeing no improvement she felt that she was no longer able to travel across to keep cleaning their house as well as her own, she herself had small children. Doris also informed social services about them. Doris was a lovely clean hard-working lady and hated to see her small nephews and nieces in such a state and the house in a filthy state again despite all her hard work and sacrificing her time when she had her own house to keep clean, but years later still felt some guilty about it which she shouldn't have done. The condition of the children and the house also led to the GP and Vicar working with the NSPCC to try to support and advise Jack and Sheila to change things. Eventually they were warned that he needed to go to work and that they needed to look after the children, keep them clean, feed and clothe them and to clean and look after the house otherwise they could lose the children, but things didn't improve so the children were then removed from the house and taken into care under a Place of Safety Order. Maggie the youngest child was only 4 months old. Jack and Sheila were both charged with Child Cruelty and Neglect and were subsequently both given custodial sentences for this at the court in Rotherham, the court records and newspaper article about the case can be found in Rotherham reference library. The four children John, Shirley, Kenneth and Margaret (Maggie) on being taken from the house were separated immediately. Maggie was hospitalised immediately, she was very poorly. John and Shirley can remember some of this period of their lives and they continued to miss each other from the day they were separated. They never lived under the same roof again. Likewise, Ken missed Maggie even though he was only a small boy he would ask for Maggie frequently, again they never lived under the same roof again. Sadly, Maggie passed away very suddenly in her 50's so all we have of her are a few memories as Shirley and Maggie didn't come into our lives again until they were in their late 30's. I didn't meet them until later as I was living abroad at the time they contacted the family. Shirley had wanted to have contact with John again and Maggie with Ken. I will discuss them in more detail later.

Returning to our situation, five and a half years after the incident of being told by my Mum that I had to go and live with Jack and Sheila, Mum had to sit me down and tell me that I had to go and live with them in a place called Chesterfield. That meant nothing to me at all, I didn't remember being told that I was to go and live with these strangers and I didn't know where Chesterfield was at all why would I? I had never been there to visit. During that five and a half years there had been a few visits to the children's offices in Rotherham to see Jack and Sheila but quite often they did not turn up. Some people were at the children's offices on one occasion and I was a little scared of them. They didn't interact with us at all and I don't think the man even spoke to us, they just sat there staring as May, Irene and I played with each other. My Mum, May and Irene's Mums as you may recall were often informed that meetings had been planned but then on arrival at the children's offices were informed that the meeting was not going ahead as they hadn't turned up. On occasions our Mums were informed by our social workers not to tell us that they were going to be there as there was every chance that Jack and Sheila wouldn't turn up again and the social workers didn't want to confuse us.

Now however, because I could read and write independently and some things had been put in place for our return to Jack and Sheila, (I will discuss these later as May and I found out the truth years later) I was being encouraged to write letters to Jack and Sheila I had to write Dear Mum and Dad at the beginning of the letter and then write about what I had done at school. Sheila wrote back saying how much she and Jack (Dad) and the boys; Tommy, Robert and Dean, were looking forward to May, Irene and I going to live with them. I never wrote a reply saying that I was looking forward to living with them or even May and Irene. It still didn't fully register with me that I would really have to leave my Mum, Dad and Ronnie. I certainly didn't want to even though I was continuously being informed that May and Irene would be living with me too by Miss Short and my Mum. My life was with my Mum, Dad, Ronnie and my extended family and friends in Maltby I was quite happy with things as they were, and I was quite happy seeing Irene every Friday and May occasionally. I knew May and Irene fairly well but at that point we were more like cousins than sisters. Each of our Mums had supported each other at different times during the time we had been with them. I had stayed at Mays home when my Mum went into hospital for an operation and then convalescence for a couple of weeks and I even attended May's school during that time. When I stayed with May we were told off because their stupid dog ate the beautiful little animal's that we had made from plasticine and had left on the hearth over-night to dry, the stupid dog was sick, I thought that was unfair as we didn't make the dog eat it. The dog should have been told off for stealing our animals. We also both got told off for making too much noise when there was a funeral on the television that we were made to watch. It was Winston Churchill's funeral, we didn't know who he was at all and had no idea what a funeral was. Irene stayed with me when her Mum had a baby and she came with us on a day trip to Cleethorpes. That was very eventful, Irene and I slept in Ronnie's double bed and she was sick in the night, all over the bed and her nightie and mine. Mum had to change both of us and the double bed, then wash the bedding and our nighties. We had a nice day at the seaside and Irene bor-rowed one of my swimming costumes a nice red one, Mum must have been worn out. It was nice staying with May and having Irene stay with me, but it was more like having a friend or a cousin stay over than being sisters as they were only brief visits. Our foster families were different, they were different people. I was used to being the only girl with a big brother, May had an older sister and brother and Irene had an older sister, brother and a younger sister, we were integrated into these families and as every family is different the daily social interaction is unique to that group of people. We were all naturally closer to them by this point not each other, seven years is a very long time in a child's life especially during their formative years. Irene had only been a year old when we were taken into care and we didn't see her again until we were all fostered as she had been put into the nursery at Oakwood Grange Children's Home. Our Mums met each other at the children's offices and agreed to keep all contact thankfully.

We didn't know at that time that we had two older sisters Shirley and Margaret and two older brothers John and Ken. May and I discovered only a few years ago that Shirley and Margaret had lived at the same time as May in Wath. They only lived a short walk away from where May lived but they didn't know of each other's existence then, no one introduced them to each other. Shirley and Margaret moved away to Pateley Bridge before their paths crossed as if they had remained May would potentially have attended the same secondary school as them both. Preparations for our proposed return included visiting a place called Swinton to meet our older brothers John and Ken. We had never met them before as they had been taken into care before we were born. Later when we were older, we discussed this May remembered meeting Ken at the children's offices and that we tormented him. I don't remember that at all. Maybe it was May who did the tormenting! As she had loads of practice under her belt with that by tormenting her brother Gary and I remained shy and cautious when strangers were around. John and Ken lived in a small children's home with an Auntie and Uncle overseeing it but hadn't been living there together very long and previously had not seen each other since being taken into care. Miss Short collected Irene and I after school one day and we went to have tea with John and Ken, their 'Auntie and Uncle', the people they lived with and the other children who also lived there. We were told that John and Ken were our brothers, but I don't think either of us really understood this at all. I personally had a brother his name was Ronnie I didn't need any more brothers. It still didn't really register with me what was happening, I was nine years old and Irene was eight.

We didn't visit John and Ken again at Swinton the next time we saw them was in Chesterfield at Jack and Sheila's. May, Irene and I had all spent more time with our foster brothers and sisters and extended family than each other and had never met John and I certainly couldn't remember meeting Ken previously. It was confusing that we were going to be living with these big boys and other people that we didn't know and a witch!

Following the visit to meet John and Ken, Irene and I were taken by Miss Short to visit Jack and Sheila for the day. I remember that day very well. I think that may be due to the stress I was being put under and being very wary of strangers. May had by this time already moved in with them as had John and Ken. Tommy, Robert and Dean (they had had a tenth child by then) my youngest sibling who was about two years old also lived there. They had also had an eleventh child, but he had died within a few hours of birth as he had been born prematurely. Sheila had been given a hysterectomy, if she hadn't goodness knows how many more babies she would have had. They had ten children in fourteen years. When Miss Short drove off from the house I felt overwhelmed by it all, being left with all these people I didn't know, I felt that we had been abandoned by Miss Short and wasn't sure if she was really coming back for us. I had thought that she would be staying with us all day, I had never been left with them before, my Mum was always close by and now she was miles away. It had been a long way in her car from my house and if she didn't come back I didn't know how we would get back. It was lovely seeing May of course and she looked after us all day from our arrival until we left. Jack didn't really speak to us and Sheila didn't make much effort either. May still insisted that Sheila was a wicked witch and rode a broomstick, this made it even more real as May lived here all the time and would know for sure if it was true. I was frightened that Sheila's face would change when it became night time. I looked for the broomstick in the room but didn't see it. I found out later that her face did change and her eyes when she was angry. May said the little boys were annoying but John and Ken were okay. Fortunately, it was a nice day, so we didn't have to stay in the house and we all went off to visit the Queen's Park this is a large park that is in the centre of Chesterfield. We all walked there, Jack was a heavy-set man (he weighed around 14 stone) and always walked with a swagger, the style that men who are full of their own self-importance use. Shoulders back, head tilted up and back just a bit too much and stomach (his stuck out a bit too far). When we got to the entrance of the park we had to stop as there were men on the gates selling tickets. There was a cricket match being played, Derbyshire played at the Queens Park sometimes and on this day, they were playing there so if you wanted to go into the park you had to pay. You couldn't just access the lake and play area then as it wasn't fenced off in anyway. To say I had my eyes opened at that moment would be an understatement, Jack was furious at being informed that he would have to pay to go into the park, his quick temper was soon in full flow. Him being a big solid man made him more threatening (later we nick-named him Fat Jack) as he grew in stature at that point by pushing his chest out and straightening his body more which increased his height. I hadn't heard some of the words he used but I knew they were not nice ones due to the reaction of people who were also waiting to go into the park. The men on the gate tried to calm him down and asked him to mind his language as there were ladies and children present. Jack carried on ranting and raving, but the men stuck to their guns and said rules were rules, there was a match on and he would have to pay an entrance fee to get into the park. We didn't go in as he wouldn't or couldn't pay for us to get in and the air continued to be blue for the rest of the day. I think on looking back that it says much about him as a person that he had no thought whatsoever about how his behaviour would affect two small girls that didn't know him. I cannot remember him speaking to either Irene or I at all on that day and he certainly never demonstrated any affection to us and neither did Sheila. I learnt over the next few years that it was never Jack's fault it was always someone else at fault that he had a very quick temper and would become violent and lash out at any-thing or anyone in his path. May informed Irene and I to ignore Jack that he was always swearing and bad tempered. Irene was eight and half, I was nine and half, May was almost eleven I had never seen anyone act in such a way and neither had Irene and before living there May hadn't either. I, as you may recollect got smacked for singing 'bloody' it wasn't just the swearing it was the body language and the way he shouted that was extremely frightening. Neither he or Sheila thought of taking us to another park in the area and we ended up following him back to the house with him still swearing and then continuing to be in a bad mood for the remain-der of the day. To say I wasn't impressed with Sheila is an understatement as a child I compared her to my Mum. My Mum was clean and kind and spent time talking to me. Sheila was dirty and smelled of stale cigarettes and she didn't talk to us or even hold our hands as we crossed the main roads when we had walked to the park and back to their house. She didn't demonstrate any mothering behaviours towards us, May fulfilled that role. At the end of the day Miss Short collected us, we didn't dare tell her what had happened especially as we would have to tell her the words he had said and then we might get into trouble. We were already frightened of this man who we had been told we had to call Dad.

A few weeks later, Irene and I had to stay for a weekend visit. I was dreading it, what if that man, Jack started shouting and swearing again, I didn't like him, I was frightened of him. On the weekend visit that Irene and I made there was no visit to the Queens Park or any other park to make up for the disappointment of the previous visit, in fact Jack and Sheila didn't take us anywhere. We were sent out to play with the rest of the children, I had never had so much freedom to go where I wanted without an adult. Also, I didn't have to change into playing out clothes so that my best clothes would be kept clean. Of course, Irene and I didn't know the area at all, so we followed the other children. Sheffield Road was the main road from Chesterfield to Sheffield at that time and was always very busy, there was traffic all night long and the bus depot was across the road, so we were woken up early from the constant noise of the early morning buses constantly going from the bus depot. It is interesting that Jack and Sheila had the quietest bedroom at the back of the house. There were two more bedrooms upstairs. The room next to Jack and Sheila's was occupied by the boys. John had a single bed and then Ken, Tommy and Robert slept in a double bed in one of the rooms. Dean slept with Jack and Sheila. He slept with them until he was about ten years old. Our room was at the top of the stairs on the right-hand side. To the left-hand side there was a small landing that led to two further bedrooms. May and I slept in a double bed and Irene slept in a single bed in our room. There wasn't any carpet on the floor and the curtains were very thin in our room. There was a small cupboard and a cabinet in our room. There was a sash window that we could open to get fresh air, which was needed as on the small landing at the other side of the stairs that led to the boys and Jack and Sheila's bed-rooms there was a tin bucket that the boys urinated into during the night rather than going to the toilet down-stairs. The stench was awful especially during the summer months as Sheila didn't empty it very often. On one occasion someone kicked it over, we girls got out of the house as quickly as we could on that occasion, no way were we going to clean that up. We went downstairs if we needed to go to the toilet.

There were some derelict houses across the road from Jack and Sheila's. They were due to be knocked down. As you will understand, derelict houses are not a safe place to play in. Jack and Sheila didn't supervise us at all, we children went into those houses to play, Tommy and Robert who would have been seven and five years old had a great time smashing windows and anything else they could break. May, Irene and I watched them and then after a while we went with May for a walk, she said the boys are stupid. The boys got absolutely filthy, their faces and hands were black with the dirt and sticky in places, but they didn't have a bath before they went to bed, my Mum would have scrubbed me, I would have been in serious trouble for getting dirty like that. Again, on that weekend visit Jack and Sheila didn't demonstrate any affection to either of us or spend any individual time with Irene and I to get to know us or us them, in fact I cannot remember if Jack even spoke to us the whole weekend. It was May and the boys looking after us and talking to us. To say I did not want to go and live there is an understatement. In my care notes it says that 'Iris is the more refined of the Allcock children and there are concerns about how she will fit in'. None of us that had been in care 'fitted in', that environment was alien to all of us that had been in care. We had all been looked after and cared for. We had always been given regular meals, sat around a table and were clean and dressed nicely. I couldn't remember living with them before and I had hardly seen them in over seven years. We were used to living in clean houses with people who went to work, were not bad tempered, violent or used foul language. The people we lived with were clean in themselves and looked after us, they spoke to us, played with us, took us to visit different places and knew exactly where we were and doing.

May at eleven was already doing the housework that Sheila should have been doing. Our bedroom was clean and tidy when we went on the visit and after we moved in, May had made it as nice as she could. The rest of the house wasn't clean, but May couldn't bear to live in such dirty conditions so she scrubbed the floors and did the washing using a washing machine with a mangle. Mays arm even got trapped in the mangle on one occasion before Irene and I went to live there but Jack and Sheila didn't take her to the hospital to make sure that she was okay. Once we went to live there the three of us, May, Irene and I would take all the children's washing on a Sunday afternoon to a laundry about a mile away to wash and dry it. Jack and Sheila's washing was done separately. May had looked after Irene and me on the visits and when we went to live with the family she continued to do that, even at the age of eleven she was like a little mother, I knew this just wasn't right but at least May gave Irene and I some protection and calmed us down during and after Jacks outbursts. As I have stated there was no affection demonstrated towards Irene and I by Jack or Sheila, they didn't hug or kiss us or even show any pleasure that we were with them at all or towards any of the other children apart from Dean the youngest. He carried on sleeping with them in their bed until he was about ten years old and was allowed to do whatever he wanted. During the visits and after we went to live them Jack behaved in his normal way, and lay on the settee as he watched the television. I had not looked forward to living with them at all before I had to, I was right not to. My care notes don't say that either. They just state that I had enjoyed being with May for the weekend visit at no point did Miss Short or anyone from social services sit Irene or I down to ask anything about the visits and how we really felt about leaving our foster families, going to live with Jack and Sheila or what we had done when we were there. There are no notes following our removal from our foster homes and how we were settling in within our new environments, I don't think social services were interested in the slightest despite Jack and

Sheila's history of not showing any interest in us, not attending arranged visits, not signing documents for medical appointments or inoculations.

The day I had to go and live in Chesterfield with Jack and Sheila was one of the hardest of my life and it certainly was for my Mum. I still didn't really understand it all though, I wasn't able to comprehend that I would not be coming back after a few days. Especially after we had very little contact with Jack and Sheila for over seven years and very little with the children that we were also to live with. On two of the occasions Jack had displayed violent outbursts which he had also done at the children's offices in Rotherham. Not knowing them other than on the recent visits when he had been very bad tempered, aggressive and had used words that if I had repeated I would have been in big trouble also that he didn't even speak directly to any of us was bizarre. Miss Short arrived to collect me, my belongings were packed into her car. I cried big tears I didn't want to go to be with that man or woman. Mum was trying her best not to cry she reassured me that she would see me soon as Jack and Sheila had agreed I could return to Maltby during the school holidays I think this was in part due to Mum being persistent in attempts to keep in contact with me. Mum gave me a big hug and a kiss and put me in the car, we spoke of it years later and she said she should have fought for me like Shirley and Maggie's Mum had, they never returned to live with Jack and Sheila. I don't blame Mum for it at all as it was beyond of her control and as I was growing up I said that to her. Mum stood on the road waving until we were out of sight. Miss Short then drove to Irene's house and her belongings were packed in the car and we set off. On route we were taken for a medical, from that day on we never had another annual medical like the ones that we had during the time we were in care when we were being well cared for by our Mums.

I cannot remember being taken into care at the age of two, I clearly remember being taken off my Mum at the age of nine and half that day. It was absolutely horrendous, I still feel upset about it now. I don't know how my Mum coped with her daughter being taken off her to a place that she had never seen and being handed over to people who she had seen for brief moments especially when he had been shouting and bawling at the social services staff, banging on the desk with his fist and that she, May and Irene's Mums had been asked to take us away from the children's offices in Rotherham to get away from him. If I had been her I also would have been very worried about me going to live with them. In fact, if it had been me now I would have done anything to prevent it, but hindsight and maturity is a great thing and times were very different then.

When we arrived at Jack and Sheila's or 'Sheffield Road' which we all usually refer to the house as, I never say 'when I lived at home' when referring to that place, our belongings were unpacked from the car by the boys, Sheila, May, Irene and I and put into the house. Miss Short make a speedy getaway, she didn't come into the house or go to our bedroom with us to make sure that we were settled and inspect it like she always inspected my home and room in Maltby. When I think about it I find that bizarre, why did social workers 'inspect' everything in our foster homes and the care that we received but appeared to ignore the fact that we were being placed into a strange environment with people that had criminal records for child cruelty and neglect and therefore should have carried out the same inspections. The day Miss Short left us with Jack and Sheila was the day that was the last time I saw Miss Short. Irene and I were in for a rude awakening but at least Irene and I had some protection in the form of May, John and Ken. May had not had anyone when she had to go and live with them before us. May had been the first to be returned to Jack and Sheila.

Chapter Five

Traumatic Times

On our arrival at Jack and Sheila's the day we were supposed to live with them forever. The younger boys; Tommy, Robert and Dean were fascinated with the toys that Irene and I had brought with us and helped to carry them from the car to the house. Many of the things were quickly broken by the three boys over the first few days so we quickly learnt to keep our precious items safe in the bedroom that we shared with May. Jack and Sheila did nothing about the damage to our possessions the boys were not disciplined about it or made to apologise. Some of mine and Irene's possessions had been put into a tall cupboard and we never saw them again! The possessions that I never saw again included a gold cross and chain given to me by my cousin Sheila, the silver bangle I received when I had been a bridesmaid for May's foster sister Linda, and the cup that I was bought when I visited Sooty in Southport. These items of Irene and I had been very precious to us and we treasured them, so why remove them from us in the first place, why didn't they allow us to keep them in our room so that we could still see them and wear them? Where did they go? They were probably sold by them. Jack and Sheila appeared completely ignorant about how Irene and I might feel about removing our belongings, the boys breaking our things and being separated from the only family that we had known for over 7 years. We were told by Jack and Sheila reinforced it that we had to call them Mum and Dad. Jack even raised his voice and shouted those other people have never been your Mum or Dad and shouted that we shouldn't have called them that and them F**** social workers shouldn't have let us call them that. We were made to feel that we had done something wrong. We wouldn't let the younger boys into our room after they broke some of our things and it helped that they were scared of May. The boys had also broken some of her things including Tommy cutting her favourite doll with a knife making a vagina!

The house was extremely scary or rather Sheila made it scary for us. It was what would be called a link detached house and to the other side was wasteland that contained many trees, it was a bit scary coming back to the house and walking up the drive in the dark. It had previously been an undertakers home and business. At the end of the drive there was a detached garage that was let out to a man who kept his car in there for quite a long time, Jack didn't like the man keeping his car there, he was quite rude to the man, he stopped using the garage and Jack was able to have it then. The house was large and was an L shape. From the back of the house to the far right there was a two-storey workshop where the coffins had been made and stored. Jack kept chickens and rabbits in there, which led to vermin especially rats, this was reported by the neighbours and he had to get rid of the chickens. He also stored his motorbike in this building but if he had any work to do on his motorbike he would wheel it into the kitchen where it was warm due to the fire being lit to take the motorbike apart and mend it. He didn't clean the kitchen afterwards and didn't appear to notice that we needed access to the sink or anything in the kitchen. May when she was older had just finished scrubbing the red terracotta tiled kitchen floor and Jack took the motorbike in there, May lost her temper with him and he took the motor-bike into the scullery, there wasn't of course a fire in there to keep him warm. The scullery was next door to the kitchen and had a sink in there and the one and only toilet, we didn't have toilet paper, we had to use news-paper to wipe ourselves, there wasn't a lock on the door either so May, Irene and I would guard the door from Tommy who had a habit of deliberately opening the door if one of us was in there. The kitchen was a large room with fireplace and a fire was sometimes lit in there. There was a drying rack for clothes that was pulled up above the fireplace. There was a large white pot sink that was always cluttered with dirty pots but that is where we had to wash ourselves and brush our teeth, if we girls were having 'strip washes' the other two would guard the doors so that the boys couldn't come in any of them. There was a gas cooker that was always covered in grease and a cabinet that was always cluttered with different items and sticky as it hadn't been cleaned after it had been used. There was another room downstairs that was full of clutter and smelled of damp. This room wasn't used until later when we cleaned and tidied it up so that we could go in there and listen to John's records and dance after he had bought himself a record player. It had a separate door to the outside so had probably been the chapel of rest when

the house had been the undertakers. In the living room
which was always dark and gloomy, there was a heavy
square table in the middle of the room with a few chairs
around it, a large sideboard, a settee to one side of the
fireplace and an armchair at the other side of the fireplace. We children often made the fire in the morning as
it was so cold. John taught us how to make the fire as he
worked on different shifts so wasn't always there to do
it. We made paper sticks out of old newspapers, found
a few wooden sticks and used some coal. When we lit
the fire, we had a few near misses when we used a piece
of newspaper over the front of the fireplace to create a
vacuum to draw the flames, as the newspaper caught
fire we had to quickly push it onto the fire and became
quite adept at this, recognising when it was about to
catch fire. As far as I am aware the chimney was never
swept so the room always smelled sooty mixed with a
horrible fusty smell. There was no Mum here in this
family home getting up early in the morning to light the
fire, prepare breakfast or make sure our school clothes
were clean and ready, we did it all ourselves.

The scary bit about living there was created by Sheila,
there were three doors in the living room, one led into the
kitchen, one to the stairs and another door from that
accessed the pantry and steps down to the cellar. In the
cellar was where the gas and electricity meters were, the
coal was stored there, it was dropped through a grate at
ground level in the back yard. There was also a large
stone slab in the cellar. Sheila informed us that the slab
was where the undertakers had laid out the dead bodies
and educated us all about ghosts, well her version of
ghosts. We were absolutely terrified and continued to

be terrified of going down into the cellar, Sheila demanded that we went down to put money into the electricity or gas meter when the meter ran out, she wouldn't give us a torch or any sort of light to go down the stone steps and help us to see to walk across to the other side of the cellar to get to the meters. We had to feel the wall which helped guide us to the gas and electricity meter and then on our return journey we had to also feel for where the stone steps started to get back up to the room door. Sheila then took great pleasure as she locked the cellar door behind us once she had heard the coins had been put into the meter after first shouting things down to us to make us even more frightened. It was pitch black down in the cellar and combined with the stories she had told us about the slab in the cellar being used for dead people and ghosts we were very scared. Sheila really enjoyed hearing whichever child it was getting upset you could see it in her eyes and her facial expressions. When May and I got older we refused to go down to the cellar and Sheila had no choice than to go down herself as Jack was due to return and he would not be pleased if the television wasn't able to be put on for him. So, after shouting at us 'I will tell your Dad you wouldn't put the money in the meter' she went down to the cellar to do it as we still refused to do it. Once she had put the coins in the meter we did the same as she did, shouting scary things and making ghost noises and locked Sheila in the cellar she did not like that at all and banged on the door, swearing at us and shouting that she would tell Jack of us. We were now of an age where we didn't take any notice of her threats, May had already stood up to her on a few occasions from being about the age of fourteen. Sheila could have gone down to the gas and electricity meters herself during the day to put money in them as there was natural light into the cellar during the day from the grate where the deliveries of coal were made. She appeared to enjoy upsetting and frightening her children you could see it in her eyes. Interestingly Sheila never did that to us when Jack or John were at home.

In the September after moving to Sheffield Road, Irene and I were taken to our new school; Christ Church Primary School to register. I was quite nervous as I wouldn't know anyone other than Irene and she wouldn't be in the same class as me. I missed my friends from the Crags school so much. It was only a short walk away so after the first day we used to go to walk to school and home by ourselves. We had to get ourselves up and ready for school, of course there wasn't any breakfast for us to start the day. May had been to the school for a few months the previous year so had informed us that it was very nice there. Tommy and Robert were in the Infant classes. May moved onto Secondary School that September so she had to be up early and catch the school bus from across the road at 8.25am to get to Edwin Swale Secondary Modern School in Whittington so May was the one who woke us up for school every morning. We relied very heavily on May organising us all. Neither Jack or Sheila got up to give us breakfast or make sure there was anything for us to eat. Our first meal of the day would be our school dinner which was often free as Jack wasn't working due to him having '*lazyituss*'. They always remained in bed until late in the mornings. Sometimes they were out when we got in from school they often went to Bridlington or

Cleethorpes for the day leaving the back door unlocked so that we could get in, that was kind of them.

My first teacher at Christ Church School was Miss Fox. Her classroom was in a prefabricated building behind the school hall which was where the children did indoor PE and ate their dinners. Everyone had to walk down the hill from the main school building at dinner time and back up the hill afterwards. Miss Fox didn't have much time or patience for children especially if they were slow learners. She knew how to use a ruler to rap children's knuckles or would slap them on the back of their legs if she became frustrated with them for not knowing something especially the multiplication tables. Fortunately for me I was a quick learner and could already read, write and do all the basics in mathematics and always practised multiplication tables and spellings so she never got the opportunity to rap my knuckles or slap my legs. School was my escape, it was my sanctuary it meant I wasn't at Jack and Sheila's, they couldn't do anything to me if I was in school and I wouldn't have to listen to him shouting and swearing if he was angry about something. Fortunately, I had always loved going to school from the day that I had first started school and always worked hard as I wanted to know everything. The following year was my last year at Primary School I remained at Christ Church School and went into Mrs Sanderson's class, she was a lovely lady, she always had a smile for everyone and she made lessons fun and interesting, she didn't use a ruler other than to draw lines and measure things. She treated all the children alike and grouped them according to ability for some lessons. I thrived in her class especially as she had a wonderful selection of books and she encouraged me to read stories such as Alice in Wonderland, Alice through the Looking Glass and Enid Blyton's books. After I left Christ Church School she had a baby, I made the baby a fluffy Gonk and took it to her and Mrs Sanderson was really pleased with it. I took the 11 plus we sat the tests in the building where we did PE and ate our school dinners. The tests didn't worry me and I passed but Jack and Sheila wouldn't allow me to go to the girls Grammar School which was quite close to where we lived, Jack said that they weren't going to be spending any f******* money on me going to a posh school after Miss Hanbury the Headteacher had informed them that I had passed the 11 plus so I could go to the girls grammar school but that they would have to purchase some items for me. Due to their refusal to buy anything for me to go to that school I attended the same Secondary Modern School as May. They didn't pay anything for our school uniforms though, they managed to get school grants to buy these for us.

Out of school we played out in all weathers or just roamed the streets, we got to know the streets and most of the areas of Chesterfield and beyond very well. No one asked where we were going or what we had been doing and if they were told what we had been doing nothing was said. We even played on rope swings, swinging over Chesterfield canal which was quite a dangerous thing to do. We often went into town and used to go into the Parish Church; the Crooked Spire a great deal, it was warmer in there in winter, we didn't have hats, scarves and gloves to keep us warm or boots. We did play with some of the local children who were similar ages to us occasionally but some of them were very rough and were bullies. They loved to fight other children just to prove that they were hard. One girl called Lesley picked on May for quite a while when she was with other girls but not when she was by herself as was May. On one occasion when this girl was again with some of the other children she continually goaded May, she went too far, May became angry at being bullied but it wasn't until she hit May that May hit her back in fact May floored her, in front of all of Lesley's friends too. The girl's parents called the police, they were informed about the girl and that for weeks she had been constantly threatening and picking on May when she was with the other girls. The girl admitted that she had been doing that and never bothered May again in fact we hardly ever saw her again as she didn't go to the same school as us and I don't think she ever walked past Jack and Sheila's again. Ken was a very quiet boy and very gentle, none of us had been brought up in families where people were aggressive or swore. A boy beat Ken up once after he had been bullying him for a while. Jack told the younger ones to look out for the boys Dad, Mr Johnson coming up the road, he was only a small man and when he was walking up the road he got the shock of his life Jack walked down the drive onto the pavement and beat him up. This was supposed to show Ken what to do if someone hit him. It was okay for him and Sheila to beat their children but not for others to do it. Strangely enough Mr Johnson didn't call the police, he was probably too frightened to.

In late October we earned some money by building a guy and waited outside the local pub asking for money from the men as they came out of the pub. Sheila asked us for the money, we didn't give any of it to her we bought food and sweets for ourselves with it. My Mum was appalled when I told her about what we had done, she told me to be careful asking for money from men outside the pub and not to do it if I was by myself. My Dad didn't say anything more about it until years later. Whenever I told her what had happened since the last time that I had seen her she didn't make any negative comments as she was worried that Jack and Sheila would stop me from seeing her. My Mum did tell my Dad though and we spoke about it all when I grew up. We children also went around singing carols knocking on doors across Chesterfield and did this night after night and did quite well with this enterprise. We could then go to the chip shop and buy supper for ourselves. Irene and I did a newspaper round each but didn't do very well as we couldn't get up on time as we weren't allowed an alarm clock so that only lasted for a few weeks. I think it was amazing that we always managed to get up on time for school. The paper round was just far too early for us then.

Irene and I had never washed our own hair before we went to live with Jack and Sheila. Sheila never offered to help us bathe or do any of our personal care that we had been used to having done for us. May taught us how to do these things. Sheila never demonstrated any maternal skills at all not even to the younger ones. My hair had always been put into ribbons everyday by my Mum, there was none of this at Jack and Sheila's. I have never met a woman with a daughter who has not wanted to dress them nicely, even girls who have been 'Tom

Boys' as they are growing up, dress their children nicely and include pretty things for their daughters. I continued to have my hair cut in Maltby at the hairdressers my Mum went to every school holiday when I returned home for a week, two weeks or the six weeks summer holidays. I would also return to Sheffield Road with clothes and other items my Mum had given me.

The bathroom that contained a bath, a sink and a sideboard was accessed by walking through Jack and Sheila's bedroom, their room always had clothes strewn all over the floor. May, Irene and I always went into the bathroom together May went in the bath first, she said she was cleaner than us! Then it was my turn and then Irene, I think it would maybe be called the pecking order. May would make sure that Irene and I had washed all the shampoo out of our hair completely otherwise she said we would get dandruff. She also always making sure we didn't have 'dickies'; head lice, although Irene did get them once. When waiting for our turn in the bath or after we got out we would spend the time jumping off the steps that went down into the bathroom onto the beams in there and we would swing and climb on them for ages like monkeys. When we had finished in the bathroom it was the boys turn. Tommy, Robert and Dean they had to use the same water that we had used. They always complained that the water was cold but never said it was dirty so all three of us must have been clean after all. Jack and Sheila ignored their complaints. Luxury items like nice soap were not bought we used dark green fairy soap which was really for cleaning the house not your body and toothpaste wasn't initially bought as Jack and Sheila both had false teeth. We experimented with salt and even the dark green fairy soap that we washed in. Eventually May managed to persuade Sheila that we needed toothpaste and some smoker's toothpaste was bought as it was cheaper.

Jack used to cut Ken, Tommy, Robert and Deans hair, he would shave most of the boy's hair off and then he would also cut Irene's hair in a basin cut above the bottom of her ears. It was a cruel thing to do to Irene. Once she was old enough Irene grew her hair long and still has long hair, it is so long that she can sit on it. Cutting his children's hair so short was cruel particularly in the winter. Why would he think it appropriate to cut his little girls hair that short? He never cut May's or my hair at all I don't know why, maybe he was worried about what May's and my Mum would say. I always had my hair cut during the holidays whilst in Maltby. John was working by then, he went to the barbers, Jack never cut his hair. Sheila sometimes cut Jack's hair, he went to the barbers sometimes too. He didn't have his hair cut so short as his young sons. Jack nicknamed Ken Dopey and he called me sparrow legs, specky four eyes and any other swear words that came into his mind he even frequently said that I didn't need glasses and only had them for attention. I had attended the Optometry Department since I was four for a squint in my left eye and to correct my vision. The forms to give permission for me to attend the Optometry Department were one of the forms that Jack and Sheila had been chased up on repeatedly to sign so that I could attend there. Interestingly Jack didn't call John or the other children names. We girls called him 'Fat Jack' but not to his face. None of his daughters liked him or Sheila.

May didn't like school and Sheila regularly allowed her to stay off to clean the house and do the washing. As I have stated she got her arm trapped in the electric mangle on one occasion but was never taken to hospital to make sure that she was okay, why would you not take your young daughter to the hospital to make sure she was okay? Sheila never cleaned the house, she didn't work outside the home and neither did Jack very often. As I have stated neither of them got up in the mornings before we went off to school so we didn't have any breakfast. When we were in primary school we were grateful for the school milk in the morning and the school dinners that were free when Jack wasn't working which was most of the time. When we got back from school it was pot luck what was available to eat most of the time. We even had sugar on bread and margarine as there was nothing else available, Sheila however still had her cigarettes that she chain smoked and Jack went to the pub all day on a Saturday after the Giro had been cashed. Sheila didn't work, even if she had been at home all day she hadn't done a thing including not making sure there was something for her children to eat and didn't care in the least about this. The beds all remained unmade although we girls did make ours before we left for school as we had been brought up doing that in our foster homes and our bedroom was always clean and tidy. We didn't have much but what we did have we looked after carefully and still do. I had always kept my Mum informed of everything that had been going on when I returned home during the school holidays. Once when my Mum returned me after the school holidays Sheila moaned to her that I would not do the housework. My Mum informed Sheila that I always cleaned my own bedroom when I was at her house, made my bed every morning and did other jobs. Sheila said, 'I think she is expecting to have her own lady's maid'. My Mum didn't respond, she already knew that May stayed off school to do the housework and that Sheila didn't do any of it herself. On Tuesday afternoon there was a small box of groceries delivered by the Payne's this was a couple who owned a small shop across from the field where Jack and Sheila had lived in the bus. Tuesday was a good day when we arrived back from school we would have a treat a bag of crisps that we used to make a sandwich. That box of groceries didn't last very long.

Occasionally Sheila would cook a huge pan of corned beef hash that would last a few days. Jack however wasn't happy about his children having the corned beef hash particularly if we had had a school dinner he thought that was enough for us. On one occasion when he returned from wherever he had been Sheila served him a plate of the corned beef hash that we children had also been served and were eating. In a temper that came from nowhere he threw his full plate at the wall the air was blue with his foul language about us eating the same as him and that we had already had a dinner at school, he kicked one of the little ones out of his way as he stormed off. He had huge issues about his children being fed at home I could never understand that and still can't. A parent would not eat anything without asking their children if they would like any of it and they would then share it with the children. Even animals feed their young first why didn't he?

Despite Jack not working most of the time and there-fore not bringing any money into the house he always went to the pubs in town most Friday nights and all day on Saturdays. We have spoken about this over the years and think that he spent the family allowance on himself and any other benefits that he received by not working. On Saturday mornings by about 10 o' clock the routine was that Sheila would cook him a huge piece of steak bought at the local shop, this was cooked and served to him by Sheila then he would get dressed up in a nice suit, shirt and tie and highly polished shoes. He also had a nice warm overcoat for the winter and a hat, scarf and gloves to keep him warm. The pubs didn't stay open all day then so May and I or one of the others would have to go to the Midlands bus station café in Chesterfield town centre for about 5 o'clock where he would be having a break from drinking alcohol and would be sat eating and drinking tea with a group of men and women who wore makeup including bright red lipstick and had nice clothes and hairdo's but who all smelt of alcohol from their dinner time drinking session. We had to go to meet him there in all weathers to collect the bags of fruit that he had bought off the Saturday market for himself. We had to take it back to the house and put it in the alcove to the side of the settee where he lay most of the time when he was in the house. We children were not allowed any of the fruit or the fizzy pop that he also had in this corner of the room hidden from view. He would sit and stuff his face with fruit and drink the pop in front of us all, we wouldn't dare look at him or his temper would flare up. He sometimes gave Dean the youngest child some of the fruit, he would rather it go bad rather than him sharing it with any of us. Once the pubs opened again for the Saturday evening he would be back in them drinking until closing time. Sheila didn't make us go to bed, there was no set bedtimes or routines, we would stay up and watch television. Sheila would say 'your Dad will be back soon, have a look to see if he is coming, if he's in a bad mood get to bed quick'. As you can imagine Jack was always drunk on his return and this could go in any direction, if he was in a good mood he might occasionally bring chips back for everyone. If any of us were in bed we would be forced to go back downstairs and eat the chips that he had bought. He could of course be in a foul temper and then he might upturn the heavy wooden table with all its contents, milk, sugar, cups, plates flying all over the room because we were still up. He also pulled the heavy old-fashioned wooden doors off their hinges when he was really angry, he even smashed the television up on one occasion. We children would scarper quickly if he was in a temper as he didn't hesitate to lash out with his hands or feet and he didn't care who was on the receiving end of his venom. Other than when he went to the pub he always wore heavy duty motorcycle boots that fastened up the front with laces, if he kicked out at a child, the child would physically fly up into the air. Jack was selfish, lazy, ignorant, bombastic and had very low living standards for his wife and children but always managed to eat, drink and dress well himself. The family allowance and any benefits were spent on his own gratification, they wanted John back as he was working and that meant more money coming into the house. Also due to the child benefit they would get for us that meant an even bigger income for themselves and their own gratification. Sexual intercourse had been a good long-term investment for them. They never sent any money with me when I went back to Maltby for all the school holidays, they never bought me a Christmas present or a birthday present either at any point of my life. Irene informed me recently that the only present that she ever received at Christmas was from a charity when she was there with them. John recently informed May, Irene and I that Sheila frequently asked him for more money as well as the money that he had already given her for his board. She informed him that she needed to buy clothes or shoes for 'the lasses' as we were referred to. We informed him that she didn't buy us anything. Ken was there when we were discussing this and informed us that she had also asked him for money citing the same reason. Both John and Ken did not look happy at the information that we gave them, the reality of Sheila lying to them to get more money from them when Jack had been so visibly selfish over the years must have hurt and made them cross.

If the washing machine wasn't working on Sunday afternoons May, Irene and I had to take all the washing except Jack and Sheila's to the laundrette as we would all need clean clothes for school on the Monday. They had already served prison sentences for child cruelty and neglect and part of that had been the filthy undressed state the children were in. Sheila could have done the laundry herself during the week and at the weekend but no, she was far too lazy and instead she made May, Irene and I struggle and carry the large bags of washing on a Sunday afternoon in all weathers to the laundrette. We became quite adept at getting the washing dried in the tumble dryers and managed to save some of the coins and bought ourselves sweets with them. If the washing machine was working at Sheffield Road, then May always did a lot of the washing when she stayed off school and later when May was working Irene stepped into her shoes and stayed off school to do the housework and washing. When Sheila had informed my Mum that I refused to do the housework. She didn't say that I refused to stay off school to do the housework or that she never did any herself. I don't know who washed Sheila and Jacks clothes presumably Sheila, but I was never aware of her doing it. Apparently, the school bobby often called at the house about May and Irene being off school, they went back to school for a short while but then stayed off school again to do the housework. No one appeared to follow things like that up either despite Jack and Sheila's history.

May, Irene and I didn't have the amount of school clothes that we needed for a whole week so we always kept ourselves clean by handwashing our school blouses and other clothes during the week, at one point we only had two pairs of white socks for school so would wash them out by hand and then put them in the oven to dry as we thought that it would be quicker, a good plan for clean dry socks except for the time when the socks melted due to the nylon in them. I think John bought us some more, If he was there, May used to get John to wring everything out for us by hand as he was stronger than us, the items would then dry quicker, we would also use the clothes airer in the kitchen that was attached to the ceiling above the fireplace, our clean clothes were then dry by the following morning ready to iron. We survived and kept ourselves clean despite having a lazy slovenly mother. None of us liked being out and about with Sheila and if we spotted her before she saw us we hid from her.

We were not allowed the light on in the living room, I had to complete my homework in the television light during the darker nights. I sat on a chair at the table as close to the television as possible squinting at the homework as I did it. Jack would often say what the 'f***' is she doing? Sheila would stick up for me about having to do the homework and how much I had to do every night. The others didn't get homework or very little of it. One night when he had returned, Sheila had prepared him something to eat, I was totally engrossed in doing my homework and he shouted, 'hey you specky four eyes get me the F****** salt' I replied out loud instead of in my head without looking at him 'get it yourself, you are nearer to it'. He quickly stood up, his chair toppled over, he was about to hit me, he was furious, his fat face was bright red. May quickly grabbed the bread knife off the table and said 'you touch her, and you get this' as she pointed the knife at him. Amazingly enough he went and got the salt swearing and saying things like 'I don't believe it, cheeky b****** it comes to somat when kids don't do what they're f******* told'. He never ever hit me or kicked me, if he had, he probably wouldn't have stopped and I wouldn't be here to tell the tale. He absolutely hated it that I could read, write and had passed my 11 plus. After he had failed his driving test, (he did drive a car for years without a licence but probably thought he might get caught) he returned home and said that the test was stupid, Sheila asked him why they had failed him, he replied 'I didn't know what these f******blue signs with lines were'. I piped up 'were they white diagonal lines? Three lines, Two lines and One line? Jack said 'yes'. I said they are the countdown markers on the motorway telling you how far it is to the exit'. He called me a clever f******* b******* and I should have done the test instead. I was only fifteen then but did pass my driving test the first time a few years later. He probably hadn't even read the Highway Code....

We were not allowed a light in our bedrooms, there was a little amount of light from a street light but on dark winters morning three girls getting ready for school in the dark was not good. Jack did however let us have a red lightbulb for a while as he said it was cheaper than a regular one! May then found out that red lights were used by prostitutes to let customers know they were ready for business, the light bulb was quickly removed by her. Getting dressed in the dark winter mornings were interesting if we hadn't sorted our school uniforms out the night before as we were all about the same size. May then managed to get us candles for our room, Tommy and Dean would whine about us having a candle in our room but we told them to shut up and we kept our candles. Although May, when she was fifteen and working, nearly set the room on fire one night when she couldn't be bothered to get out of the bed to blow the candle out and Irene and I refused to get out of bed and do it. May sprayed the hairspray she had bought herself at the candle thinking it would extinguish the candle like throwing water on it. It went whoosh, she didn't do that again and fortunately nothing was damaged. It was scary but also extremely funny. The bedroom certainly lit up brighter than it had ever been! Tommy who frequently spied on us shouted 'Mum the lasses have set their bedroom on fire'. We shouted, 'No we haven't, he's lying again'. The bed May and I slept in was very old as was the sprung mattress. One night when I jumped into bed I cut my leg on a spring that had come through the mattresses fabric. My leg bled quite a lot, but they didn't take me to the hospital. My leg was sore for days and I had a scar for years. The solution that Jack and Sheila came up with was to put a flock mattress on top of the one with the spring sticking out. A flock mattress is filled with small bobbles of black wool. The height of the bed increased so much we had great fun trying to get into the bed and would run and jump to get onto it. Irene had a single bed and she even managed to hide the fact that she had a pet mouse in our room for quite a while as she slept at the other side of the room. She called the mouse Bobby as he repeatedly bobbed in and out of her pocket when she carried him around. Bobby died after Sheila found out and made her put him outside. Although we were being neglected and mistreated we still had some fun together.

Sheila always looked dirty and her breath smelled of cigarettes, she was always poorly dressed unlike Jack who always wore clean clothes. Although neither of them would work other than Jack going occasionally to the pit and neither of them would clean the house. She always had money to chain smoke and he always had money for food for himself and booze, a motorbike, a car and nice shoes and clothes. The most common reason he gave for not working was his sinuses were playing up. I have inherited sinus problems, you take a paracetamol and go to work. Even though he had never passed a driving test Jack had cars, vans and motorbikes that he went out and about in during the day. He went out a lot during the week even if he wasn't at work due to his 'sinuses playing up'. He would buy and sell items, where he got them from is anyone's guess. The items included clothes, he never provided Sheila or his children with any of the clothes he had. Our school uniforms were bought by claiming a grant and our foster parents continued to buy clothes for us. May's Mum even bought bras for her as she didn't have any and she had developed so much that she needed them. When May returned to Jack and Sheila's following the school holidays Sheila asked her what she was wearing, May replied a bra, and Sheila called her a slut for wearing one. Why she would lash out at her young daughter in such a way about wearing a bra is beyond belief, she should have been buying May bras. When each of us started our monthly periods, she broadcast it to all our brothers and Jack. It was extremely embarrassing for us and as Tommy was horrible to us about it, we all used to hide being on our periods the best we could.

Jack may not have provided food and clothes for his wife and family, he did however provide Sheila with garden canes. These were for her beat us with and she did so frequently but again like locking us in the cellar she didn't do it in front of Jack or John. She didn't need a reason to cane us it was something that she enjoyed doing. That kind of behaviour exhibited by her was even more reason for us to be out of the house as much as possible. When Sheila decided to cane us, it was also one of the times when the expression in her eyes and face changed. She became the evil witch that May had said that she was. Her eyes were staring and wild looking and her facial expression was sharp with her lips pursed forward or her mouth open with her false teeth clenched together. On one occasion Jacks youngest brother Brian came to visit. Jack was out, Sheila began showing off to Brian and demonstrated to him how she kept us in order, she chased after us around the table and room hitting whichever one of us she could with the cane. If you have ever been hit with a cane you will know that it leaves two red lines either side of a white one and it hurts a great deal. Brian never said anything about it or made her stop he probably didn't know what to say. These beatings happened for quite a few years and the canes were replaced when they split at the end. Of course, we all grew taller and when May became the same height as Sheila she snatched the cane out of Sheila's hand and threatened to hit her with it. May then broke the cane up across her knee in temper and threw it onto the fire. Sheila shouted, 'wait until your Dad comes back I will tell him, he will go mad'. May shouted back at her 'tell him and I will tell him that if he buys you another one I will hit you with it and him'. Even if she did tell Jack, Sheila never used a cane on us again and we never saw another one. Considering how May reacted on this occasion I think it was understandable as she was the one who stayed off school and cleaned the house, she was spending a great deal of her time running the house as an adult would whilst the person that should be doing it did nothing, May was in the adult role and not Sheila.

A man paid a visit to the house once, he cornered May in the kitchen, and May thought that he was going to touch her inappropriately, May being quick thinking picked up the poker and threatened him with it and then ran into the living room and told Jack and Sheila what the man had tried to do. They didn't bat an eyelid, they completely ignored the incident. If someone had done that to my daughter I wouldn't have ignored it, they would have been dealt with. The man never visited again that I am aware of, if he did May and I were out. We consider ourselves to have been very fortunate that we were not subjected to sexual abuse.

The secondary school that May, Irene, Robert and I attended was Edwin Swale Secondary Modern and did not have corporal punishment when we attended, children who had misbehaved were put on conduct sheets and had to see the Headteacher at the end of each day. School was great compared to being with Sheila who enjoyed hitting us and bullying us. Sheila could also be very violent without the canes. Poor Ken was at the receiving end of her venom on many occasions, on one occasion. He had had a bath and she claimed that he still had tide marks (where the dirt had not all been washed off) she instructed May, his younger sister to go and bath Ken. May refused to do this of course and Ken was obviously upset about it. What a bizarre cruel thing to ask May to do to her older teenage brother. They refused and so then Sheila beat Ken with a yard brush, she kept hitting and hitting him repeatedly, he couldn't have escaped as he was up against the living room wall in between the kitchen and cellar doors, he was cornered. Ken was black and blue on his torso she appeared to be very accurate and knew how not to mark Kens face and hands when she repeatedly beat him. Her eyes were piercing, she didn't appear to blink at all, her face was all twisted just like the witch May had described to us. We were all shocked and absolutely terrified, the look in her eyes were of a wild woman. I had never seen such cruelty and brutality and fortunately have never witnessed it again. Sheila hitting us with the cane was bad enough, this was much worse it was a full on beating. She repeatedly raised the broom above her head and brought it down heavily onto Kens body. Sheila only stopped when she became too tired to continue. The following day in the PE changing rooms the teacher noticed the marks on Ken's body and asked him about them. Sheila had obviously not thought about the chances of being found out. Remembering that Jack and Sheila already had been in prison for cruelty and neglect it is incredible what happened next. We, the other children were asked about the incident by someone who came to the house, they may have been a social worker, Jack and Sheila however were present in the room when we were spoken to, we couldn't speak as openly as we may have if they had not been present and were not able to defend Ken to the extent that we should have been able to. We were all still shocked and frightened that she might do it to us. The next thing I remember is that Ken was removed from Sheffield Road as though he had done the wrong thing and he went to live in a children's home in Holymoorside. Being an adult now and being more informed we should have all stuck together and if any of us had been beaten we should have reported it. I apologise to Ken as I should have been braver. Social services from scrutinising everything in our foster homes and having annual check-ups failed us. They sent us to live with people who had been to prison for child cruelty and neglect and then abandoned us. There was a social worker that visited the home, these visits were usually when we were at school and even if we were at home we were not asked how we were. There were five of us that had been removed from foster care to live with Jack and Sheila, one of those five was placed back into care due to being beaten and one of the younger children placed into care too. Even when there were incidents such as Ken being beaten they mishandled it. It was assault and now as an adult I would say Sheila should have been charged with assault. May and Irene stayed off school because they didn't like going to school and Sheila didn't like to do housework she had a track record of this, that was also neglect of her parental duties. There was no 'proper' follow up of supervision of us by social services. Tommy was removed from Sheffield Road after he had moved to a different Secondary School to the one we went to, we never found out why he was removed from Jack and Sheila's care.

I continued to love going to school and worked hard, it continued to be my refuge. Children from parents like Jack and Sheila were not supposed to be academically able and they certainly didn't know how to support one that was. They never attended parent's evenings or any performances that we were in. Irene and I were in a school production one year and it was Ronnie's sister in law, Maureen who came to see us in the performance. I was in the top set for everything throughout my time at Edwin Swale and loved it. We continued to have free school meals and at Secondary School we had to endure the humiliation of queueing with the other children that were on free school meals but at least we received a hot meal on school days. When Jack did go to work then we were not allowed a school dinner he said they were too expensive, we were given a small amount of money and bought a bag of chips and sat in the local park whatever the weather and ate those.

Secondary School was brilliant for me I loved most lessons especially English, I even became a Librarian and even learned how to repair books including any spines that had been damaged. My love of sewing increased I learnt how to use a sewing machine. The first item that we girls all made was a hymn book cover. Everyone was give a hymnbook on the first day of school and had to hand it back on the last day of being at the school. Many hymnbooks disappeared close to the last day of the school year as some of those leaving the school had lost their hymnbook at some point and wouldn't receive their final report without it. The second item that we made was an apron and cap for cookery lessons. These were made in the colour of the house you were in and we had to embroider our name across the top of them in chain stitch. My apron was blue as I was in Brook house. Music was another lesson that I enjoyed although it could often be spoilt by the silly behaviour of some boys. A teacher visited the school weekly and taught pupils how to play instruments. I auditioned to play the flute and was successful so learnt to play the flute and was in the school orchestra playing hymns for assemblies and occasionally during other events such as parents evening so that parents could see what we were learning. Science was fun especially when we could use mercury and had it rolling all over the bench. Maths was good but spoilt by the teacher. Although corporal punishment wasn't used in the school. Mr Wilson, who was also the Deputy Head would throw the chalk or the wooden blackboard rubber or smack pupils across the back of the head if he thought they weren't paying attention. He smacked me across the back of the head on one occasion as I was staring at the board and he thought I was daydreaming, I was actually trying to understand the problem that he had written on the board. Sheila had to pay a visit to complain to the Head Teacher, another Mr Wilson as my ear had bled onto the pillow during the night and the GP asked me after he had looked in my ear if I had been hit on the head. He didn't hit me again, you could always tell who had been in his lesson by the chalk marks on their blazer. Interestingly, Jack didn't go and sort Mr Wilson out like he had Mr Johnson, who hadn't done anything. My other favourite lesson was Art by Mr Towse, I thought that he was very talented. My brother Ken is, and my sister Maggie was talented at drawing, I wish I could be half as good at it as them.

Following on from May however and especially after she escaped on her sixteenth birthday and returned to her Mum and Dad in Wath upon Dearne I had become braver over time as I had grown taller and was able to speak up for myself. When I was fifteen I started working on a Saturday at Woodhead's Café in Chesterfield as a waitress, this enabled me to buy my personal care items such as sanitary towels, soap, toothpaste, tights, things I needed for school such as pens and pencils along with the money that my Mum provided me with to be able to return to Maltby at the end of each school half term.

A schoolfriends Mum, Mrs Lye gave me some of her daughter's clothes including summer uniform dresses. She said they were things that Jackie had grown out of, I think some of them may have been new. So along with the clothes John and my Mum bought me, my sister in law Sheila and those clothes my Mums sister made me I was okay for clothes and other items throughout my time at Jack and Sheila's. May, Irene and I also visited some Jehovah's Witnesses who taught us about their beliefs. They also gave us clothes. Irene and I are not Jehovah's Witnesses but May joined their congregation as an adult as did her husband.

May and I often visited Sheila's Mum our Grandma Wass. She worked full time as a cook at Scarsdale hospital, May had been named after her. Her name was Doris May Wass she was a very kind lady and always made us welcome, her house was clean just like the ones we were used to . Grandma would make us a drink and give us something to eat and talk to us both asking us how we were and what we had been doing. She would also give us some money to buy sweets. Grandma Wass would talk to us about the past and our other relatives on her side. Grandma Wass' maiden name had been Whitton and the family had lived at Sheepbridge. We met her Dad and her brothers, sisters and nephews and nieces. They all lived in nice clean houses and were also lovely people and were always very welcoming when we knocked on their doors. We often visited these relatives for somewhere to go away from Jack and Sheila. May stayed at one of Grandma Wass' sisters, Auntie Winnie's occasionally when her granddaughter was visiting from the south of England. We were constantly thinking of places to visit rather stay at Jack and Sheila's. Sheila had two brothers and a sister called Iris which is where my first name came from. They didn't have anything to do with Sheila, Jack or us. I remember Grandma Wass and Auntie Iris visiting once but they never visited again, Jack was very rude to them and he never went to visit Grandma. I don't think they were impressed with the state of the house. Sheila would visit Grandma Wass most Saturdays. Once when Sheila was out visiting Grandma Wass, May gave the younger boys a good bath and dressed them in clean clothes. The boys complained about this and May was told off by Sheila for upsetting them. It was amazing, Sheila never thought to bath them herself or keep them in clean clothes.

Grandma Wass was divorced from Grandad Wass they divorced after Grandad Wass left Grandma Wass with four children. Sheila was their eldest child she had not been the best-behaved teenager. Sheila had worked in a chip shop after she left school and had apparently begun training to be a hairdresser. She then started seeing a married man, Jack, and got pregnant to him, Jack already had a baby daughter to his wife. Sheila did inform May that Jack had been married before, she didn't inform May about the whole story. Their marriage certificate proves that he was. Grandma Wass had not been happy with that at all and had thrown Sheila out of her house, but then had Sheila and the baby lived with her for a while before Sheila ran off with Jack him leaving his wife and child behind. People may try and say it was due to her broken home that she behaved why she did. Well her parents didn't beat her with canes or neglect her and her siblings didn't behave like her.

She had a large extended family who were all nice hard-working people. Grandma lived with a man called George he seemed nice a quiet man. Grandma Wass worked as a cook for many years as Scarsdale hospital in Chesterfield.

Grandad Wass when I first met him he was living with a woman called Madge, he wasn't married to her, we visited their house and their house was clean too. My watch had broken once, Grandad tried his best to fix it for me. He was a very tall man, over six feet tall. Years later as an adult I began researching my birth family tree. One day I was contacted on one of the sites by several people one of them was one of my Grandad Wass' daughter from his second marriage; Julia. I then learnt not only did Grandad have Julia to his second wife he had ten children to her. Some of his children to his second wife are younger than me. When I first saw him, I thought he was an old man! One of his daughters is Rosemarie Smith. Rosemarie is a year younger than me. At the time we were all being sent to live with Jack and Sheila she and her younger siblings were being taken into care, she has written books about her childhood. Rosemarie was taken into care after her Dad, my Granddad Wass had left them and their mother. Then their mother abandoned them all. These young children lived in their family home by themselves, they didn't have any money or food. Rosemarie also suffered severe sexual abuse by one of her brothers, he was imprisoned for this. I have read her books, Little Molly and Molly II, I was absolutely appalled that my Grandad Wass had left his second family, Rosemarie doesn't blame him, she has said that in her books and to me that he was a kind gentle man. Rosemarie has forgiven her Mum and Dad for the abandonment of their children, she did suffer a great deal over the years to get to that point. Many of her friends say that she is an inspirational lady.

Grandad Wass' Mum was still alive when we moved to Chesterfield, she lived in a little cottage at Cutthorpe that was nice and clean as was her daughter's house, Hilda, who also lived in Cutthorpe they were all very lovely friendly people. This had led me to believe Sheila had no reason to have a dirty house or be slovenly. Her background was a normal working-class family who all worked hard and kept their homes clean and tidy, cared for their children in all ways including feeding and clothing them. As a child she had informed us that she had been a bridesmaid for her Auntie Hilda, we didn't know whether to believe her or not as she had told us so many lies. On doing my family history research however I found a wedding announcement in the local newspaper of Hilda's wedding and Sheila was indeed a bridesmaid for her Auntie Hilda and wore a blue dress as she had told us.

Jack's parents were also alive his Mum had divorced Jack's Dad and remarried her name was Grandma Fox when we met her but her second husband had passed away. Her house was very clean. Jack would bring her home on Saturday nights sometimes if he had met her in one of the pubs and she then slept in our room. None of us wanted to have this drunken old woman sleep with us. We thought it was hilarious that she couldn't climb onto the bed and we had to give her a push up, we had put several mattresses on it by now as well as the flock mattress we were making sure we wouldn't get cut by any springs again. Grandma Fox also wore red long-legged knickers with black lace around them which we thought hilarious. When we were laughing at her, she joined in and laughed loudly and said we were cheeky. We weren't so happy with her taking her teeth out if she asked us to put them on the top of the drawers but thought her face was hilarious when she took her teeth out she looked like a gargoyle. She didn't like Sheila at all and called her a dirty ***** even to her face. When she stayed over Grandma Fox would do some cleaning and cook a meal. She occasionally had May or Tommy to stay over at her home and she always made a fuss of them. Even though she drank too much her own home was very clean and tidy and she was very clean herself.

Grandad Allcock still lived in Thurcroft he had remarried, his wife seemed to be nice. Their house was also clean and tidy, he had worked all his life. I visited their house once when I was off school ill, Jack and Sheila took me in the car he had at the time he wouldn't let me sleep in bed or lay on the settee even though I had a high temperature. Grandad's wife took me to the shop and bought me some sweets as Jack wanted to speak to his Dad. Grandad Allcock visited Jack and Sheila's on one occasion when I lived there but he didn't visit again he wasn't impressed with the condition the house was in. Jack was his usual aggressive self about the visit as Grandad had said something that he didn't like. Jack also had siblings and they all lived in nice clean houses none of them appeared to like Sheila. May used to go and stay with Jacks sister Doris occasionally, Auntie Doris still lived in Dinnington, May was a similar age to Auntie Doris' daughter Maureen.

May and I were lucky in that our foster Mums had managed to get Sheila to agree to us going back to our foster homes during school holidays and that is what I did until I was sixteen. I wasn't allowed to call my Mum and Dad that anymore I was told I had to call them Auntie Mary and Uncle Clag. Mum said to me once after I got upset that I had to go back to Jack and Sheila's after a school holiday 'pretend that you are at boarding school and that you come home for the holidays' and that is what I did. I think it helped me cope with living with Jack and Sheila. Jack and Sheila never took me to my home in Maltby I had to catch two buses by myself apart from the first couple of years when my Mum met me in Rotherham as I got off the Chesterfield bus. Mum always took me back to Chesterfield on the two buses unless Ronnie was available to give me a lift. Mum always came into Sheffield Road every time she took me back and years later she told me how she hated leaving me there and would cry on her way back to Maltby that she had left me there. If Jack was in he continued laying on the settee and didn't even acknowledge she was there. Being a child, I asked her if she wanted to go down into the cellar and see where the slab was. She politely refused, and Sheila didn't want her to see my bedroom when I asked if she wanted to see it. My Mum always refused a cup of tea as she said that she might need the toilet when she was on the bus. May and I continued to be clothed by our foster parents even though we didn't live with them anymore. By maintaining that contact it meant we maintained our cleanliness and personal hygiene standards and our good behaviour as did Irene no matter how difficult things got. John was working and being the good brother that he was he bought us several items of clothing and on Fridays (pay day) mars bars, I always think of John when I see mars bars.

One day when I was about twelve I was told that I wasn't going to school that day I was going to Maltby with Sheila to see my Mum or rather, Mary. I was told that I was going to borrow a dress from the clothes that I had there as we were all going to for Derby to an interview to emigrate to Canada. Sheila had a distant relative that lived in Winnipeg in Canada and decided that we could all go and live there and that it would be wonderful. These clothes that I was going to 'borrow' were what my Mum and Dad had either bought or had made for me. Sheila didn't know the way as she had never even been to Maltby. Jack didn't drive us there, we travelled on the two buses all the way there and back in a day. When we got there, I was sent to my room, out of the way while Sheila and my Mum had a chat. I chose a green flowery dress that Sheila (sister –in – law) had made me that I would wear for the interview. Being young I didn't think about why May hadn't been taken to her Mums to get a dress to 'borrow'. On the day of the interview we all went all the way to Derby on the bus and the younger boys were bouncing all over the place on the bus and at the place where the interview was. Fortunately, we didn't get accepted. That may have been something to Jack and Sheila's criminal records regarding children or his reluctance to work. Years later my Mum told me about the visit that Sheila and I had made on that day in more detail, and Sheila and Jacks proposition to her. Mum had already informed me that Jack and Sheila had agreed to let me be adopted by my Mum and Dad on several occasions but at the last-minute Jack always refused to sign the papers. On the visit to 'borrow' a dress I had been sent upstairs so that Sheila could tell my Mum that Jack would sign adoption papers if she and my Dad gave them £1000, Jack and Sheila needed money in the bank to prove to the Canadian immigration department they could support themselves and the family. They were attempting to sell me to my Mum and Dad. £1000 was a great deal of money then, you could buy a house for about £4,000. My Mum didn't agree to this, she said that she was worried for weeks that they wouldn't let me see her again, they didn't do that, Jack and Sheila liked not having to feed and clothe me for a substantial part of the year. They never offered any of the child benefit to my Mum to contribute towards my keep in any way even over the long summer holidays.

We may have been living in hell at Sheffield Road, we had an ever-increasing awareness of how wrong it all was and were determined never to be like Jack and Sheila. We have always had to fight the stigma of being the offspring of such vile people but having siblings who have experienced it means the load is understood, shared and there is always that sibling support there when you need it.

May had started going out with a boy called Mick when we were at school, when Jack was told that Mick's Dad was a lorry driver, Jack being Jack asked if Mick's Dad Alan would drive this big transit van he had bought (he still hadn't passed his driving test) to Bridlington for a day out and all their family could come too. Jack had not only bought this big van he had also bought a large dingy and he wanted to go sea fishing. Alan agreed to come along, he drove the van, Jack insisted that he sat in the front alongside Alan. Alan's wife Audrey was heavily pregnant at the time but wasn't allowed the front seat, she had to sit in the back of the van on a cushion. Sheila was in the back of the van to along with six of us and Audrey and Alan's three children. No seats for any of us, we were just all scattered around loose in the back of the van along with the dingy. When Alan parked the van, it had to be near the boat access to the sea. Jack got the dingy inflated and then we children had to carry it into the water. The dingy was an old lifeboat from a boat and had a cover over the top, the whole thing was very heavy. There wasn't an engine on the dingy, Jack made Irene and I who were very good, strong swimmers push the dingy from the shore into deep water. Irene and I went to the swimming baths every weekend and spent hours in there as well as going swimming with school for weekly lessons. We could dive down to twelve foot and swim along the bottom for ages. We had no fear of the water in the swimming pool at all. However, swimming in the sea pushing a large dingy out to sea with a big man, a woman, three children and fishing tackle on board is quite hard work for two young girls, I was fourteen and Irene was thirteen. There were no lifejackets for any of us and Jack even had the audacity to complain that we weren't going fast enough. He wanted Irene and I to push him out at least a mile or more so that he could fish. The whole day was about him going fishing on this dingy that he had bought. Did Jack help? No, he was even wearing his normal clothes including a jumper not even his swimming trunks. He must have thought that he was the captain of a ship and we were the crew. We carried on swimming and pushing for quite a while, we were a long way from the shore. We then said we had had enough and swam all the way back to shore. Thinking back this was extremely dangerous Irene and I could have been swept away by a current. Irene and I then spent the rest of the day on the beach with Alan, Audrey, Mick, his brothers and May. After a few hours when the tide was beginning to come back in Robert ran up to us and said, 'You've got to come and pull the dingy back in, we all said 'no, we haven't even been on the dingy pull it in yourselves'. Jack and Sheila didn't get out of the dingy and do that, Audrey said the dingy was getting closer in with the tide. Well the dingy as I have said didn't have an engine and Jack was too lazy as was Sheila to get out of it and pull it into the shore themselves, they chose to remain on it and allowed it to go closer to the sea wall and the harbour. It all happened very quickly and within minutes the dingy was in the harbour and the sea had become quite rough, the dingy was being tossed all over the place in the harbour and was even travelling up and down the harbour wall. A huge crowd had gathered to watch including Alan, Audrey, Mick, his brothers May, Irene and me. The life-boat crew were there in the harbour too trying to attach a line onto the dingy and struggling to do that. Irene cried, May said, 'why are you crying?' Irene said, 'they might drown'. May said 'at least we can go back to our Mums and Dads then'. Eventually the Lifeboat crew managed to get them off the dingy and they were brought back to dry land. Jack was angry that the Lifeboat crew refused to save the dingy. He was also angrier that they had told him off for going onto the sea in the dingy with children, he had no engine and no oars to get back into the shore. Jack was blaming us for not pulling him back into the shore, the lifeboat crew informed him that he shouldn't have expected us to either push him out to sea or pull him back into the shore, it was putting our lives at risk. He was livid and if Alan and Audrey hadn't been there I think he would have killed May, Irene and I for refusing to pull the dingy back in when we were told to. They put him straight and told him what they thought of him and Audrey threatened him that if so much as touched a hair on our head then he would be in big trouble. Audrey also sat on the front seat going home. May and I have laughed loads of times about the dingy incident especially after the following Friday night when Jack had gone out drinking. The article about the incident had appeared in the Derbyshire Times and someone who knew Jack had cut it out and stuck it up in the pub for everyone to see. He was so angry when he got back to Sheffield Road and blamed us but he still heeded Audrey's warning and didn't touch us and I think he was beginning to realise that we were older now and would tell the police if he touched us.

May, Irene and I had never settled from first being made to live with Jack and Sheila and neither did John or Ken. On one of our walks when we first had to live with Jack and Sheila, May and I were so unhappy that we decided

that we would run away and go back to our Mums and
Dads but then decided maybe it wasn't a good idea as
we would get caught and then Jack and Sheila wouldn't
let us see our Mums and Dads anymore. By the age of
fifteen May had left school and was working in the
Co-op shop, she had to give Sheila quite a lot of what
she earned, she managed to save up her bus fare and
escaped back to her Mum and Dads in Wath upon
Dearne. Unfortunately, as she was still fifteen, and until
you were sixteen you had to remain with your parents,
the police had to bring her back to Chesterfield as Jack
and Sheila demanded it. One of the policemen told
May's Mum to give May the bus fare so that she could
come back and keep doing it as Jack and Sheila would
get fed up of it eventually, he didn't know them at all, it
was power to Jack. May of course was also earning an
income so to them she had to give them money for her
'board'. They watched her all the time after that and
she was no longer allowed to go back to Wath upon
Dearne to visit. She bided her time and the day she was
sixteen which was in August, during the school holidays
when I was in Maltby, she escaped back to Wath and
Jack and Sheila couldn't do a thing about it, she was
free at last, I didn't hear anything from May for about
three years, we didn't have mobile phones then.

May is eighteen months older than me so Jack gave me
a rough time after May left. For eighteen months he
continually threatened to make me a ward of court
telling me that I wouldn't be able to leave until I was
twenty-one. These threats were meant to frighten me
and make me stay there. They worked in some ways as I
was only fourteen and didn't fully understand the law

and I daren't speak to anyone about it for a long time. Jack was also furious that I was staying on at school to do CSE's and GCE's I was the last year group that could leave school at the age of fifteen. Irene was in the year below me and had to stay at school until she was sixteen. Jack wanted me out at work so that I could give him money as May had done. John and Ken were both in the army by that time and still sent money to Sheila, we hardly saw them although I did write regularly to John. What kind of man lives off his children's wages when they are more than capable of earning their own money? Sheila had said to me when I first started working at Woodhead's café on Saturdays that I should give her the money I earned for my keep, I refused to do that and told her that if she wanted money then she should get herself a job Her reply to that was, Jack didn't want her to go to work.

Jack and Sheila were called into school after I had made a disclosure to a teacher that I trusted about Jacks treatment of me, the violence that we had been subjected to, the verbal bullying and the constant threats that he was going to make me a ward of court if I didn't get a job and leave school. I was under so much pressure from him as well as doing my school work that I successfully applied for a couple of jobs. It was when I informed my form teacher that I was leaving school that he asked me to stay behind and he spoke to me and I then made the disclosure. Sheila attended the meeting, Jack of course didn't attend the meeting, if he had then he would have shown them his aggressive side and maybe they would have done something. I wasn't interviewed by social services about it as would be the case today. I stuck it out in that house until two days after my sixteenth birthday and then I packed a case and asked Irene to pass it on to my boyfriend when she could smuggle it out of the house I then walked out of the house and went back home. Once I was settled back home I wrote to the teacher that I had made the disclosure to and informed him that what I had told him was true and that I had no choice other than leave Chesterfield and go to where I was safe. He wrote back to me and said that he wasn't allowed to keep in contact with me but wished me well.

Chapter Six

My Escape

The decision to leave Sheffield Road was determined by Jack's treatment of me and his continual obnoxious behaviour. Although Sheila attempted to defend my decision to remain at school so that I could sit my exams it fell on deaf ears. She even attempted to persuade him that I would ultimately get a better paid job by having qualifications. If I had been born a year later like Irene, he wouldn't have been able to bully me over it as the age for leaving school was increased to sixteen, Irene had to remain at school for the extra year. All Jack could see was that I wasn't bringing in money to finance him. My intention had been to remain at school sit and hopefully pass my exams and then get a job where I could also go to college as well either during the day or in the evenings to gain further qualifications. In the third year at secondary school pupils chose and still choose the subjects that they want to take examinations in. My main choice was technical drawing this was rejected by the school and the forms were returned with a note saying that I could not have that choice as that subject was for boys and I should choose shorthand and typing. This was not acceptable to me, I did not want to learn shorthand and typing, the form was returned with a note stating that I did not want to do shorthand and typing that I wanted to do technical drawing. The school still refused to allow it and I was made to do shorthand and typing. My touch-typing skills leaned by typing to music on the big heavy typewriters alongside all the other girls have been useful over the years and I did work in offices for many years. Pitman's shorthand was a waste of time for me I never used it in any of the jobs that I was employed in and a few years later it was outdated and taken over by Dictaphones.

When I walked out of Sheffield Road two days after my sixteenth birthday Jack and Sheila couldn't have made me stay there but it was still frightening as I didn't want them to know of my plans and by not leaving on my birthday as May had done I felt I was somehow fooling them. I was still scared of Jack but not of Sheila as I had learned from May how to treat her and was now the same height as her I could also stick up for myself verbally with her. I tried to keep out of Jacks way as much as possible. Of course, I left Irene behind which I didn't want to do but I couldn't take her with me as they would have been able to bring her back as they had with May, she would be sixteen herself the following year and would then be able to escape. If I hadn't left then, I think that I would have had a breakdown due to the stress caused by Jacks constant threats. Some people now say that I am strong willed and stubborn I agree with that to some extent but if I hadn't been able to become stronger as a teenager who knows what would have become of me? As a teenager I was still frightened of my birth parents it wasn't until I was in my mid-forties that I became stronger and stood up for myself completely. John and Ken had both joined the army by the time I left, that had been their escape, they did continue to visit when they were on leave. May was back in Wath so there was only Irene, Robert and Dean living with Jack and Sheila as Tommy had been taken into care I am not fully sure why as I hadn't been there all the time he just disappeared. Tommy had gone to a different secondary school to us, I don't know why that decision was made as he was a year younger than Irene, but Robert who was younger than Tommy had gone to the same secondary school as us and not the same school as Tommy. Dean however went to Ashgate Croft a Special School in Chesterfield.

After walking out of Sheffield Road, I went to meet my boyfriend as we had already arranged. We used to meet at the Crooked Spire and when we met I told Phil that I had decided to leave and was going back to live in Maltby. Phil was aware of the bullying that Jack had been putting me through more importantly he knew my background of being in care and had visited me at home in Maltby during the school holidays by cycling there and back to Chesterfield which is about a 40 to 50-mile round trip, he knew my Mum and Dad quite well by that time and that I would be much better off there. Phil had never met Jack or Sheila or visited Sheffield Road. As far as I was concerned they were not my Mum and Dad. Phil was very accepting of the situation and agreed to meet up with Irene and get my suitcase from her the following evening for me, Irene and I thought that she would stand more chance of smuggling the suitcase out of the house. Phil and I then decided to inform his Mum and Dad; Ann and George. Ann knew a little about what I had been going through and knew my situation of having foster parents when we informed her that I was leaving she very kindly said that I could live with them so that I would be able to carry on going to school and complete my exams. They only had three bedrooms, I don't know where they would have put me, she was willing to help me stay on at school, I refused that kind offer and said that I would be going back to live in Maltby with my Mum and Dad. Ann had not had an easy childhood herself, therefore she was so understanding and was thinking of ways to help me complete my education. Phil and I then went back into the town and I caught the bus to Rotherham and then the one from Rotherham to Maltby. It was about 10.30 pm when I walked through the back door and said to my Mum 'I am home, and I am not going back' she was in the kitchen getting my Dads dinner ready, he was on the afternoon shift and due home from the pit. Mum didn't look too shocked at my arrival. When my Dad returned home from work and we told him I was back for good he asked me if I had told Jack and Sheila that I was leaving. I said 'no' he then said, 'I had better go down to the police station and let them know you are here in case they have reported you missing'. He then told me to go to bed. When I got up the following morning Mum told me that Jack and Sheila hadn't reported me missing to the police in Chesterfield. That my Dad was quite annoyed at this as were the police as it proved how little they were bothered about my safety. I then accompanied my Mum to Mrs Milnes' house who she cleaned for. Mrs Milnes was a primary school teacher at a local school but was still at home when we arrived that morning. Mum informed Mrs Milnes that I had left Chesterfield and Mrs Milnes suggested that I could maybe attend the local secondary school where her son went. I said no as they would be doing a different syllabus to me that I wanted to pay my way and that I was going to get a job, I had no intention of living off my Mum and Dad. Mrs Milnes then said to Mum that she could use their phone to ring Miss Short who had been my social worker to inform her that I had left Jack and Sheila's and that she should be able to help in some way. When Mum spoke to Miss Short it was not the response that she had expected, Miss Short informed my Mum that I was over sixteen and therefore was not her responsibility. I think my Mum thought that after seven years she knew her well and that she would have offered some support or advise her in some way. Mum had also thought that Miss Short might be able to encourage me to go to school in Maltby to sit my exams instead of work. Even now I think it is amazing that social services sent us from nice family homes to live within such a horrendous situation which we all escaped from as soon as we were old enough. After having frequent medicals whilst in care and our homes being scrutinised and reported on where we thrived we did not receive the same monitoring when we lived with Jack and Sheila. Four of us had left as soon as we were able to, no alarm bells appeared to ring, Irene wasn't visited to make sure that she was okay. I have requested my records from Derbyshire County Council social services and they have responded that there are no records. This I find hard to believe as there was some ongoing involvement with social services and I had received the same response from Rotherham social services for many years even being informed the records had been destroyed but I finally managed to get them after Maggie got hers and she was older than me. Maggie asked me to wait as she had requested hers and had been informed that she could have them so after she received hers I telephoned them and then wrote to them again and said that it was a nonsense saying they didn't have my notes when they had my older sister's notes. There are however gaps in the notes but alongside May's notes and Maggie's notes the jigsaw as they say was complete. There are however no records of the minutes that must have been taken during the meetings that must have been held when the decision to return us to Jack and Sheila were made.

Two nights after leaving Sheffield Road I rang my boyfriend Phil to see if he had managed to meet up with Irene to retrieve my suitcase of belongings, he informed me that although Irene had been able to meet up with him, she had informed him that she was not allowed to give my things to him. Jack and Sheila had said that I could not have them. The suitcase contained items that had been bought by me, my Mum and Dad and some clothes had been made by my Aunty Doreen and Sheila, even the suitcase had been bought by my Mum and Dad. I returned home from the phone box and informed my Mum and Dad what Phil had told me. Obviously, I had clothes and other belongings at home in Maltby but there was a principle involved here. Jack and Sheila were keeping my belongings and they had no right to do that as they hadn't even paid for any of them. Dad wasn't happy about this and said that he would think about it and not to worry as he would make sure that

I got my things back. On the Saturday my Dad told me to go and ring Ronnie and ask him to come and pick us up as we were going to Chesterfield to get my things.

Ronnie was married to Sheila by this time and they lived in Laughton Common, near Dinnington with their two children; Richard and Wendy. Ronnie came over to Maltby and we set off to Chesterfield. Having seen Jack during his angry outbursts I was a little worried about my Dad and Ronnie's safety, my Dad told me not to worry when I said that Jack might hit them. My Dad knew about Jack's historical angry outbursts at the children's offices and a little of what he was like but not all of it. Ronnie informed me recently that my Dad who was very slight in build, had told him that he would look after me and that Ronnie had to deal with Jack if he started being aggressive. If I had been told that maybe I wouldn't have been so nervous about going I still remembered Jack beating Mr Johnson up. When we arrived at the house I knocked on the door, my Dad said 'No don't knock on the door, just walk in' maybe he thought a surprise arrival into the house was better than standing on the doorstep so I opened the door and walked into the kitchen and then turned left immediately into the living room Jack was in his normal position laid on the settee with Dean next to him and Sheila was as usual sat on the chair at the other side of the fire. Irene was also in the room. My Dad had walked in behind me and Jack began to get up saying in a loud aggressive voice 'what the f...' but laid back down again once Ronnie walked into the room closely behind my Dad. Jack never moved again or uttered another word. With confidence I said 'I have come to get my things' and I turned to Irene who was wearing a dress that my Auntie Doreen had made me and said 'that is my dress so go and take it off and get my case and other things'. I didn't want to leave my Dad and Ronnie in the room by themselves with Jack and Sheila or indeed be trapped upstairs, I had so only escaped this house a few days earlier. For the first time in my life I had less fear of Jack but was so relieved when we left with my suitcase and belongings. After Jack laid back down Sheila started shouting and screaming, she was so angry and just could not control herself, she looked like the witch that she had many times previously, I thought that she might pick up the poker, she didn't. She was out of control and shouted, 'you don't know her, she has been in a pub' my Dad said, 'If that is the worst thing she has done after living here with you missus then she has done very well, my wife has told me all about you and this place'. Being brave I shouted at her 'You have been reading my diary, that is private, you have no right to go through my personal things'. Sheila didn't say another word, I could see she was very angry and frustrated, she was the same as she had been when May had broken the cane and threatened her that if she ever got another one she would hit Sheila with it and Jack. Irene then brought me all my things and we left. I never set foot in that house again, I did see Jack and Sheila again but in very different circumstances and they never hurt me again.

Irene and I didn't really understand about sex other than what May had told us. There was no way we were going to get pregnant even more so as that is what everyone expected of girls who had been in care. I had been out with boys in fact thirteen, I wrote their names in my school dictionary. I only went out with them for a few days or weeks and it was only hand holding and kissing I was far too scared of doing anything else. In a music lesson when the teacher had gone out of the room all the boys and girls were asking who had had sex with who. I was appalled when they asked me as I had been out with one or two of the boys in the class. The boys defended my honour and said that I only ever kissed them and wouldn't even let them touch my tits. To me they were very immature talking about sex in this way, one or two girls did get pregnant when I was at school one was younger than me and the father was a boy in my year, she had a terrible time of it and was called all sorts of names. As I have said I was going out with Phil at the time I left Chesterfield, I had first met him when I was fourteen Irene had been going to the Saturday children's club at the cinema they showed films and there was a disco during the break, it was like a Saturday morning youth club at the cinema with children and teenagers so I went along to watch the films, it was difficult to hear them though as the noise from the young people also in attendance was often deafening and also to dance during the disco. Irene began going out with Phil and I went out with one of his friends for a while called Roger. Going out meant usually meant walking around the streets in a group. Irene soon stopped going out with Phil and had a new boyfriend, that is what you did when you were thirteen go out with a boy for a few weeks and then move on. We did that usually because they wanted more than a kiss, we would not allow wandering hands at all and dumped them especially if they tried to touch us again. One night when I was supposed to be meeting Roger, Phil came to tell me that Roger didn't want to go out with me anymore, that's what you also did when you were in your teens send someone else to tell the other person. Irene did this on one occasion for me and the boy was sick all over the floor, poor lad he must have really liked me, he was a nice boy but there you go that is what happens. I was fifteen by the time Roger dumped me, Phil was also fifteen in fact he was just four days older than me. Phil was different to the boys at my school he appeared to be more mature and after he had informed me that Roger no longer wanted to go out with me he then asked me if I would go out with him. I found this nice but also confusing as he had been out with Irene, he had kissed my younger sister. I said that I wasn't sure but after being pressured by Phil a little more, including him saying 'I have always liked you even when I was going out with Irene I thought you were a nice girl' I said that I would talk to Irene and see what she said and if she wasn't happy about it then I wouldn't go out with him. If she said yes, then I might go out with him. I went home and told Irene what had happened, she said that she wasn't bothered if I went out with him or not, she didn't like him anymore and she was going out with someone else. We girls were just so fickle at that age. The following night I walked to Phil's house, he was out playing football his Mum; Ann told me where to find him. I walked up to the school field where he was playing football and when he saw me he came running over to me smiling. I told him what Irene had said and that I had decided that I would go out with him. He hugged me, picked me up and waved to the boys that he was playing football with and said that he would see them later. This was in the April after we were fifteen. A few weeks later when I met up with him he had bought me a record by Donny Osmond 'Puppy Love' and told me that was us. We saw each other a couple of times during the week as we were both busy with school work preparing for our exams the following year. At that time, I was also doing my Duke of Edinburgh Award and as part of that I was a volunteer at a MENCAP youth club. Young people up to the age of 30 with learning difficulties went to a youth club once a week, I and my school friends who were also doing the Duke of Edinburgh went every week and helped to run the youth club by doing activities such as playing snooker, cooking, dancing, crafts and just talking to the members of the youth club. Phil decided that he would like to help too, so some of his friends came along with him which was good for the young male members of the youth club. One night one of the members a young man with Downs Syndrome put his arm around me, Phil pushed him off me and told him not to touch me again. It took a while to calm Phil down, the whole thing had been totally unnecessary. At the time I put it down to Phil protecting me, his reaction had however been quite unnerving he obviously didn't understand that the young man wasn't going to hurt me. The young man was being friendly as many Downs Syndrome people are, they are very tactile and will hug people. Phil and I went on a training course for working with special needs people and continued to help even after I had completed my Duke of Edinburgh Award. I also attended a residential course at Leeds University and a group of us including Phil attended a residential course at Nottingham University when we met other people who volunteered or worked with people with special needs.

As I have stated previously Phil had cycled all the way to Maltby from Chesterfield when I was home during the school holidays. After I returned to Maltby and got a job I would ring him from the phone box (we didn't have a phone then) and we also wrote to each other every day. Phil was still at school and remained there through sixth form, we both knew how important that was. Once I moved back home to Maltby I would get a bus to Sheffield and Phil would get the train from Chesterfield, we continued to see each other at least once during the week and every weekend. We walked around Sheffield and would often sit on the nice areas around the bus station, he often sang love songs to me songs such as 'Stone in Love with You'. (That should make my children cringe.) A month after we were sixteen Phil asked me to marry him, I accepted, and we got engaged, his parents were not happy at this when they found out as they thought it was too young but had to accept it. My Mum was okay with it, but my Dad wasn't impressed either.

Ann and George bought Phil a moped and he used to come to Maltby on that whatever the weather during the week. It certainly made life easier in some ways, it was extremely cold in winter though for Phil and it would take ages for him to thaw out when he arrived at my house. He also took his motorbike test as soon as he could then we both travelled on it. After Phil had completed his GCE 'O' levels as I have stated he remained at school for sixth form to take his A levels but also worked on Saturdays to supplement the weekly pocket money that his parents gave him, so after work on Fridays I would go straight from work to stay at his home for the weekend. He later got a job cleaning the shop windows in Chesterfield which was better pay, he used to work on Sunday mornings. Ann and George were very kind allowing me to stay every weekend, but they had also been quite young when they were courting and married.

I had managed to get a job within a week of moving back to Maltby. The job was in the offices at a local knitwear factory D Byford's. Many of my relatives worked there and friends of my Mum and Dad. I did typing and copied the sheets of tickets the machinists used to demonstrate they had completed work as they were paid on piece work, they got paid for each item they worked on. I eventually became the Statistical Records Clerk. I could tell anyone where any garment was in the factory, when the orders had been packed and sent to their destinations. Maltby was a small place and most of the people employed at Byford's were either related to or knew each other. It was a lovely community to work in. I was financially independent I paid my Mum board, paid for my own bus fares to work, bought my own clothes and toiletries. I even managed to save some money. Life was good, I was back home amongst my family and friends I had no fear of Jack or Sheila, he was in the past as far as I was concerned if I never saw them again then I would be happy.

Every evening when I got home Mum would have my dinner ready just the same as she did for my Dad, she always did my washing and my ironing. Phil was always made welcome and when he walked in to the house she would make him a cup of tea to warm him up as he had been on his moped and offer him something to eat. Later that year we had to move out of our house as the council were modernising all the houses. We were to have central heating, new fitted kitchens and bathrooms, new doors, windows and fireplaces, still coal fires but the old ones with the ovens at the side were going. This was a huge investment for the council and probably well overdue. We lived in a three-bed-roomed house, the temporary accommodation had only two bedrooms but was just around the corner from Dunns Dale on Park View. After leaving for work in the morning I had to return to another house at the end of the day. In my temporary bedroom was my single bed all made up but also Ronnie's bed leant up against one of the walls. It was all a bit cramped, it was only to be for a few weeks and our house would be all posh and newly decorated when we were able to return to it, we would even have radiators in the bedrooms, what a luxury. One night I arrived back from work and Mum was a bit flustered I asked what was wrong she said, 'I have had a really bad day'. On asking what had happened, she informed me that she had been dusting my bedroom and that she had got trapped, and that she thought that she wouldn't be able to get out in time to get dinner ready. Mum as I have said dusted everything if it didn't move, she had decided that she had better dust the skirting board behind Ronnie's double bed that was leaning against one of my bedroom walls. When Mum had gone behind the bed and was dusting she discovered that she couldn't get back out, the full weight of the bed was on her and she was trapped. She then informed me that she had sworn she said, 'I said the 'b' word'. Now this was becoming quite a story Mum never ever swore. This to me was hilarious so trying not to laugh I said to her 'which 'b' word did you say?' she went all pink, blushing and said, 'you know, the 'b' word'. Continuing to keep my face straight I asked 'but which one? There are lots of 'b' words'. Mum replied, 'I can't say it again'. Unperturbed I continued, 'Go on ' I said 'tell me which one you said'. 'Did you say bugger?' Mum shook her head. So, I said 'bloody, did you say bloody?' She nodded and went bright pink again. I shook my head and said tut tut naughty girl. Then nearly wet myself laughing and she hit me with a tea towel for tormenting her. Once I stopped laughing I said, 'does my Dad know you said bloody?' She said 'no'. I just shook my head. This was far too good an opportunity to miss so when Dad came in I related the story to him. He said 'why are you cleaning behind the bed? We are going home next week.' He didn't smack her leg though like he had mine when I sang Venus in Bloody. After I had told about half a dozen people about it, when Mum was there of course, she said 'will you stop telling everyone about it'. It was so funny to me that she was mortified that she had sworn. Even now the memory of it makes me laugh, I only heard her swear once more in her life and that wasn't just 'bloody'.

We moved back into our house and it was lovely Mum was in her element sorting everything out and putting everything where she wanted them especially in the new kitchen and bathroom we also had radiators in every room we had warm bedrooms!!

Chapter Seven

Devastation

When I was seventeen, my Mum and Dad separated, it was absolutely devastating for me. My whole world was collapsing around me. There had been a few raised voices at night when I was in bed, I never thought that my Mum would leave. I didn't realise that things were so bad between them at that time, but Mum was always good at keeping things going.

Be under no illusion divorce has a huge impact on everyone involved especially the children, whatever age they are. Ignore all the rubbish that people quote; they were too young; they married too quickly; people are living longer now; you get over it; children accept it; children understand it. I think all the things people say, they say help to justify divorce and their bad behaviour. There is in my opinion no justification for adultery. You make a choice to commit adultery or not to commit adultery. If you are not happy in a marriage then sit down discuss it, try and put right the things that you are not happy with and if you can't then leave the marriage in a kind way so that you can remain friends especially if you have children. Don't bring in the additional complications and the pain that a third person brings and if you are tempted to be that third person, shame on you if you go ahead and do it.

The whole separation of Mum and Dad was made more difficult as Mum had gone to live with one of my Dad's friends. One of the worst things about this was that Mum had lied to us, she said that she was staying with another person until she was able to get somewhere else. Who would have thought it of Mum who was always so prim and proper I was furious and didn't see her for months, if she had been honest about it maybe it would have been more acceptable, you see Dad had had an affair a few years previously with the stewardess at one of the working men's club that he went to this hurt Mum tremendously. Mum asked me to go and live with her but there was no way I would go and live with the other man especially as my Dad was so devastated. He didn't like having it done to him even though he had done it himself to Mum, it was so painful to watch and be a part of. I like most children believed that my Mum and Dad would be with each other until they died, they had always been my security, my safe place. Dad soon became very angry about it and even went to their house and hit Albert, the other man. They called the police and he was told to keep away from them. That didn't calm him down he was even angrier with them. Mum even had a policeman with her when she came to collect some more of her things.

After Mum left I was in charge or part in charge of the house. Dad had never looked after the house, Mum had always done everything in the house and he was still upset and wasn't interested in eating, I took over the cooking, I wasn't that good at it, I had done baking with Mum but hadn't been taught to cook dinners, we had to eat instant potatoes, boil in the bag beef and tinned vegetables. These were absolutely disgusting and not the 'real' food that we were used to. I also bought Vesta meals, they were a precursor to the instant meals we have now. At least we didn't die of starvation. Eventually I taught myself how to cook proper meals.

One evening when I returned home from work, there was a note on the door written by Dad, it said, 'Iris do not come in'. This frightened me, I ran around to Mr Bratby's (Mrs Bratby had passed away by this time), Ian his grandson answered, Ian was a few years older than me, I gave Ian the note that I had torn off the door I was crying and trying to tell him what had happened. Ian took me into his house and asked his grandad to look after me and then he ran around to our house and then to the neighbours to use the phone and he rang for an ambulance and one of my Uncles. My Uncle Chuck came and collected me and took me to his house. I didn't see my Dad, he was taken to hospital, he had tried to commit suicide. To say that was a traumatic experience for me as a seventeen-year-old would be an understatement. I stayed at my Uncle Chuck and Auntie Doris' house for a few days and then wanted to go back home, they were very kind to me, especially Auntie Doris. The house had been cleaned up, I still don't know what mess had been made and Dad would never discuss with me what he had done. At least I didn't see it and I don't think I would ever have forgotten that image. When Dad came out of hospital he stayed with Ronnie and Sheila briefly and then returned home. Routines returned to normal or our new normal. I went to work and did the food shopping, cleaning and cooking. Dad returned to work. He still really felt very sorry for himself despite the fact he had had an affair first, so part of me didn't fully sympathise with him due to that, I felt he had made Mum do it. When he had his affair, he did this blatantly in front of my Mum and rubbed her nose in it by telling her how wonderful the other woman was. How nicely she dressed he even pretended to be asleep on the settee after he had been to the club on a Sunday dinnertime and repeatedly said the woman's name. He even did this in front of my Auntie Doris. This all upset Mum tremendously of course and I was furious with him. I did offer to leave with Mum and get a flat at that time, she wouldn't do that and said that I would soon be married and off with Phil and that would mean that she would be on her own. It was still shocking that she left and the way she left.

Other than going to the club with his friends Dads other pastime was horse racing. He always believed that he would have a big win, he couldn't understand that there was only winner and that was the betting shop owner. He was really interested in horse racing, a gambler as quite a few men were in those days. He didn't gamble everyday of course but he did spend too much money on it. At least he wasn't addicted to things such as drugs or even alcohol as that would have been every day and cost more money. It is even more amazing that Mum managed the house so well on less money than she could have had. In those days however, the wife was given housekeeping each week, that was used to pay all the household bills. Mum still bought me clothes, fed

me and gave me some money to go back to Chesterfield
with. Jack and Sheila never gave her anything for my
keep when I stayed with her every school holiday, they
kept the family allowance and any other benefits that
they got for me during my absence for themselves. I
suppose my Mum continuing to buy my clothes and
providing me with everything during the school holidays suited them both very well.

Phil and I decided that we would get married the
Autumn after becoming eighteen, we would have been
going out with each other three and half years by then.
He would have finished his A levels in the June and was
taking a year off from studying before going to university. Phil always worked very hard at his studies and
was worn out. On the day that he completed his last 'A'
level exam he arrived at my house and cried and said he
never wanted to study again. Phil had already applied
for and was successful in getting a sponsorship with
British Steel Chemicals Division as he wanted to do a
BSc in Chemical Engineering this was perfect. They
employed him for the first year after leaving school and
then during the long holidays when he was studying at
the University of Sheffield, he was able to get hands on
experience in the industry before he applied for jobs.

In the September after our eighteenth birthdays, we
married at Phil's Parish Church in Chesterfield. My
Mum wouldn't attend the wedding as things were still
very acrimonious between her and my Dad and she didn't
want him to spoil our day. My Dad was still feeling
upset about my Mum leaving and wasn't very helpful at
all with any of the arrangement or in helping to pay for it.

Ann and George were amazing and helped a great deal with the organising and paying for things for us. In fact, when I went to buy my wedding dress, I had managed to save up enough money to pay for my dress and everything else I needed. I asked Ann to come with me to help me choose the dress as well as my Mum, my Mum didn't come, she had to go to work, she was working full time by then in a factory. Ann and I had a lovely day together, it was a really hot day and the lady who dressed me in the various dresses was very helpful. Ann helped me choose the dress, headdress and a veil and as it fitted me we left the shop with it and the lady had shown Ann how to dress me and how to make sure that the train was perfect before I set off down the aisle. Ann then looked after my dress at her house and kept it covered in sheets so that no one especially Phil could see it. She had taken over the role of my Mum in so many ways since my Mum had left and I have many fond memories of time we spent together. Gran Thomas, George's' Mum was excited and crocheted some skull caps for the bridesmaids to wear, Sarah, Phil's sister was my chief bridesmaid other bridesmaids were the best man's girlfriend Lynne my younger cousin Sarah and my little niece Wendy. Sarah said she had a sister at last.

We decided to be married in Phil's local Parish Church as it was easier with Ann and George helping us to organise everything. Phil slept at his best man's house the night before the wedding and I stayed at Ann and George's. Ann brought me a cup of tea on the morning of the wedding then she and George set off to set up the Village Hall where the reception was going to be held after making sure that Sarah and I were okay. Sarah and I had a fun time when for some reason we decided that we ought to iron my veil as it looked a little creased, it wasn't a good idea at all and the iron stuck to it but there was no damage. My family came to Ann and George's house and the bridesmaids and I used the living room as our dressing room. My Mum rang me before I left for the church, that was so hard for me, I had to fight back the tears otherwise I wouldn't have stopped crying. I had always imagined my Mum and Dad being together at my wedding with my Mum there supporting me and helping me to get ready. Ann even stood in for the bride's mother and travelled in the car with the bridesmaids to the church instead of my Mum. Another negative side of divorce is the family is ripped apart and never properly being together at family events or able to chat about the past or the future of the family all that is stolen from you especially when there is a third party involved in the breakup of the marriage.

My Dad was supposed to travel to Chesterfield with my Uncle Chuck and Auntie Doris in the morning, he wasn't at home when they called for him, he eventually turned up in Chesterfield he had caught the bus to Rotherham and then to Chesterfield instead without informing anyone. So, for a few hours we had no idea where he was or if he was going to be at the wedding. In the wedding car before we left for the church my Dad said 'Are you really sure about this? It's not too late to change your mind. I think you are making a big mistake, you are not going to have an easy time with him and Ann is going to be a nightmare mother in law, you will never be good enough in her eyes for her precious son.' I thought he was being mean and I wouldn't listen to him, Phil and I had already discussed getting married and about never divorcing and I was also still annoyed with my Dad for causing me stress by not arriving with Uncle Chuck and Auntie Doris and in part that my Mum wasn't there due to his behaviour, so we set off to Church and I married Phil. The Church was full of family and friends, we had a lovely wedding day. We spent the first night in a local hotel near the railway station, Phil sneaked, fish and chips into the room, we hadn't eaten much all day as we had both been so excited and busy talking to all our guests. We went to London for a few days for our honeymoon. We had our future all planned out as you do at that age. We didn't have loads of money, but we had each other and our dreams, all was well.

Chapter Eight

The Journey into Adulthood

I have never regretted marrying at the age of eighteen and think it is pathetic when people say it is too young to get married, many marriages last when the couple have been childhood sweethearts, just as many marriages fail when the couple are much older. Age isn't the main issue, a successful marriage is built on trust and respect, understanding that you are not perfect, no one is but we should strive to be. It is about loving someone unconditionally and being selfless rather than selfish. It is about understanding that sometimes the other person may be annoying but being aware that so can you, and that you must work through any difficult times together.

Phil and I lived with his parents, and sister for six months after we got married until we found our own home. This was not an ideal situation, but we hadn't been able to find somewhere before we married in part due to Phil still being at school until he finished his exams in the June and we discovered that we couldn't rent anywhere until we both had a stable income that would guarantee we could pay the rent. Our presence must have irritated Phil's sister Sarah as we were at home a great deal and she wanted time with her boyfriend by themselves and we probably just irritated her anyway as she was sixteen years old. Ann as kind and helpful as she was, could also be very moody and was taking antidepressants at the time. Ann had not had an easy childhood, George had spoken to me about it a great deal. As I have stated I think that is why Ann had offered to help me when I left Jack and Sheila's and was so supportive after my Mum and Dad's marriage broke up. Ann and Sarah had been in a very traumatic accident a few years before, a car had mounted the pavement, due to skidding on black ice and had hit Ann and Sarah. They had both sustained serious injuries and had been in hospital for a long time, Ann walked with a limp for the rest of her life and probably permanently suffered from the injuries that she had sustained in more than the obvious physical ones I think I might have had nightmares. Ann never drove again after this accident even though she hadn't been driving, over the years I constantly tried to get her to drive again so that she would have that independence, even suggesting she bought an automatic car so that she wouldn't have to change gears and to have some driving lessons with her brother in law Ron who had taught her to drive. In part this was because there were often arguments between Ann and George and she ended up crying in their bedroom. I was always informed that it was because she had wanted to go out for a drive and George didn't want to go out. We went with them sometimes for a drive and that was what it was a drive around the Peak District and maybe a very short stop somewhere before heading back home. Ann wanted to go away on holiday, but George never wanted to go. Ann often told me that she wanted to go and see different places, she wanted to go abroad again (they had been to Italy on a coach trip a few years before) and to Belgium but George didn't want to go abroad, it took Ann a great deal of effort to get him to agree to go anywhere. Phil and I went on holiday with them to Minehead one year for a week but considering their children were now grown they didn't make the most of their new-found freedom. George passed away before Ann and after his death she discovered that he had thirteen bank accounts and that there was over £20k in one of them, she said to me 'our lives should have been so much better'. George was always worried that they wouldn't have enough money for the remainder of their lives and wanted to make sure there was, and that if he passed away before Ann she would have enough money. For the remainder of her life she bought items that she had been gone without during their marriage and went away on holidays.

Ann also bought herself a computer and used it to keep in contact with my children. I found her a book that would help her after Hannah said, 'Grandma still keeps getting it wrong when she is trying to do emails and stuff, I have shown her loads of times.' I sent Ann the book she rang me to thank me and she said it was very good. She loved her Grandchildren a great deal and was very proud of them all. When she came to stay with us she would go into Hannah's room and 'help' Hannah tidy it up, folding things up and putting them in drawers, sorting toys out and putting them away neatly. When they had finished she would say 'now then my little darling will you keep this nice and tidy so when I come again it will still be nice and tidy'. Hannah would say that she would, I think she had forgotten within a day or even a few hours. George was a good Grandad he would talk football non-stop with the boys, who was playing for who and where each team was in the different tables. He used to talk a great deal about Chesterfield getting a new all seater stadium and his punch line was, 'yes they are buying a three-piece suite'. He would love the stadium the team now have.

Before and after our wedding, Phil and I spent months looking for somewhere that we would still be able to afford to pay the rent when Phil went to University the following September as planned. We liked some of the places, George frequently advised us against them as he thought they were too far away or expensive. We even considered buying a small terraced house that we would be able to afford but George decided that wouldn't be a good idea. Thinking about it years later George interfered far too much in the management of our finances. One of Ann's brothers and his wife lived in a terraced house and knew that we were looking for somewhere to live they informed us that a house was empty. We went to look at the house and although it wasn't the nicest house that we had seen, our first home became a two-bedroomed terraced house with an outside toilet and no central heating. The house was close to the canal, I was very wary of rats being around due to people informing me they lived in the banks of the canal. There were about six houses in each yard where we hung washing to dry and if we were at work and it rained one of the neighbours would get the washing in for us. The front of the house had a small garden and there was a footpath that led to each of the houses, to the other side of the footpath was a company; Bryan Donkin that was busy twenty-four hours a day, it was noisy during the summer especially as we had our windows open. Before moving into the house, we decided to continue to live with Ann and George whilst we cleaned the house up and redecorate it, some friends and family came to help us. We didn't have much of a clue what we were doing and when the brickwork on the chimney breast started coming away when we were stripping the numerous layers of wallpaper off we quickly stuck the bricks back in and the layers of paper back on and papered over that. The ceilings were also in such a poor condition Phil's Uncle suggested that we cover them with polystyrene tiles. Phil's Uncle and George stuck them on the ceilings for us, that was a huge improvement. We bought a gas water heater to get instant hot water and a gas fire for heating. We also bought an inexpensive three-piece suite, a bed, wardrobe, dressing table, flooring and curtains. We had all the essential items as I had been buying them since we had become engaged and we had received many items as wedding presents. Family gave us other pieces of furniture and we had a home of our own.

Phil worked for a year and then commenced his studies at the University of Sheffield travelling to Sheffield each day on the train. Initially I had found a job working in a glass factory 'Dema Glass' in Chesterfield but within the first week of being there I successfully applied for a position in the offices at the Kennings Tyre Services depot on Brimington Road, Chesterfield. This was one of my favourite workplaces during my working life, like Byford's it was like working within a big family environment. Even though Phil and I didn't have very much money we managed to get by. To earn more money I sold cards, makeup and items from catalogues. I made my own clothes, and even made a suit for Phil. I also knitted many items including jumpers for both of us. We both even made presents for people at Christmas and birthdays. One year, Phil made wooden planters and I made things by sewing and knitting them. We couldn't afford to go out very often but were quite happy with that as we were both working for our future. Phil along with some schoolfriends had formed a band and this continued after we married they practised during the week and then played a few gigs for which they got paid for. Lynne and I were often the first up on the dance floor trying to encourage the other people at the gig to get up and dance. This was some of our social time as we would have a drink or two at the gigs.

When we were living in the terraced house and Ann and George were visiting us one evening George answered the knock on the back door, he knew the man at the door and began talking to him. The man was a local councillor and was canvassing for votes in the upcoming local council elections. George asked the man 'when are you going to get these two rehoused?' Central Terrace where we lived was due to be demolished as part of a redevelopment program. B & Q is there now along with other out of town stores. During their conversation the man said he could get us rehoused and asked which of the new estates that were being built did we want to live on. We moved soon after that into a brand new two-bedroom council flat. What a luxury that was. We had an inside toilet, a bath, a fitted kitchen and gas central heating. I also had more customers to sell makeup to as there were a lot of young families on the estate, I spent many evenings delivering the makeup catalogues and knocking on doors collecting the orders and then packing up the orders, delivering them and collecting the money for the orders. Even though money was tight we managed to hire a car from Kennings Car Hire for a week and we stayed in a flat in Scarborough for a week, on another occasion we hired a car and went out and about for days. Phil still had the moped so that was our usual mode of transport. We had to be very careful and not waste money but knew that the sacrifice of going without things that our friends had and did was going to be worth it in the long term.

Towards the end of Phil's degree when he was applying for jobs we needed a car for him to travel to interviews. We managed to buy an old Ford Escort by selling the moped. It was great having our own car we even took Phil's Grandma out to the pub one night, she loved it and there was a great deal of laughter. Gran Thomas was a very tiny lady and had been nicknamed as a child 'Dolly' by her Dad this name stuck, her nieces and nephews always called her Auntie Dolly. She was born in Ramsgate in Kent and would often talk about her childhood there. She had met her husband Samuel in Ramsgate during the first world was when he was stationed there. Gran Thomas had had a tough life being widowed early with two young children and had never remarried. She could be very stubborn and difficult at times but was also a very kind lady. On New Year's Eve she was 'in charge' of midnight and would insist that George did the first footing as he had dark hair. Everyone would be laughing as she was so determined that it all had to be done at precisely the right time and she would be telling George it was time to go outside into the cold night air over and over again until he went outside. The door then had to be closed and then he had to knock at the right time, there was always confusion about whether it was on the first chime of Big Ben or the last but by the time Gran Thomas would allow him back into the house the last chime must have rung. When we left to go home she would say 'you make sure that you go into their house first to George as Phil's hair was too light for Gran Thomas's superstition'. Poor George had to walk up two flights of stairs when we lived in the flat just to do the first footing. He couldn't disobey his Mum even though she wasn't there. She might have been a little lady, but Lillian Rose Thomas was an amazing lady. She is one of those people that has been a part of your life and the memories that you have of them always makes you smile or laugh. It was quite fitting that our youngest daughter was born on what would have been Gran Thomas's 90th birthday.

Gran Thomas moved to Chesterfield after she had married. The Thomas family lived in Sheepbridge which is also where my birth mother's family, the Whitton's lived and George knew them all especially my Great Uncles who played in a band at many of the social functions around the local area. George had also played in a band for years, he was in a works band, they had all had a mutual interest in music and would be at the same social functions. I have a photograph taken at a street party and George and his sister Evelyn are on it alongside some of the Whitton family. My Great Grandad and his brothers had also served in the first world war alongside George's relatives. It was amazing that I married someone whose father knew my 'nice' birth family relatives.

Phil continued to go to Sheffield University on the train and I went on the bus into Chesterfield until we bought a car then I went to work in the car. One day I popped out to do the shopping at dinner time unfortunately I hit someone else's car and damaged the wing of our car. Phil went ballistic with me. shouting and swearing at me I was really frightened and burst into tears he then shouted at me 'don't you dare cry, that is emotional blackmail'. I felt so bad about damaging the car anyway I hadn't done it deliberately I was a new driver. Phil didn't speak to me for ages he could be moody like Ann. A few months later Phil ran into the back of someone's car on a roundabout and guess what I didn't go ballistic I said, 'these things can't be helped, they happen.' He said that made him feel worse because he had shouted at me so much. Ah well that tells a tale in itself he knew he shouldn't have shouted at me in that way. It had also brought back memories of Jacks rages, totally unnecessary and uncalled for. Another occasion that I saw a side of Phil I didn't like was when Phil was at university. He always wanted me to take a day's holiday from work to go with him to get his results which I did it was in a way Phil including me in his successes. The day that his final results was fabulous, he had gained a first-class honours degree, the Tutor said they had never had anyone get such high results. He had also been awarded some of the annual prizes for his course. This was it, we had reached a target, Phil had got a very good degree. All the hours of studying that he had done had paid off. I was so proud of him as was everyone else. He was however, extremely rude to his parents after he had received his final results. We were going to see Gran Thomas in George's car on the Thursday night as was usual and they were both really pleased about his results as any parent would be Ann mentioned putting his results into the local paper 'The Derbyshire Times' as many parents did. His response to this was extremely surprising and he said to them in a very firm voice, 'don't you dare brag to anyone about my results. It is down to Iris that I got my degree.' I was really shocked and upset that he hadn't appreciated anything they had done for him, or for us both. Before we had got married had informed Phil that if we married they then they would not support him financially at university and that had caused a great deal of upset but they did a great deal for us they had transported us around all over the place in their car, they had helped us organise and paid a substantial amount towards our wedding, they had even let us live with them until we had found somewhere to live and had even bought him a new suit to go to interviews. They had fed us loads and also helped with practical things like decorating. I didn't understand how ungrateful, uncaring and disrespectful he was being to them, I was really upset about it. He had been given everything since the day he was born, they weren't wealthy but lived in their own house and had both worked hard to make a secure future for their children. They had both lost their own fathers at around the age of five or six, so life had been very tough for them in so many ways. Ann especially was so proud of him, she had problems conceiving children and so from the day that Phil was born she had put him on a pedestal totally devoting herself to him, she thought the sun shone out of his backside. She was always saying how clever he had been as a small child and had been in the class the year above his own age. With Sarah however, who was not quite as academically bright as Phil although she was a clever girl she had never quite measured up to Phil in her Mum's eyes. Sarah was very much in the background from day one. Ann was really hurt by his outburst, I should have spoken out, but I chose to keep quiet as he had that determined look on his face that said, 'I have decided, I am right, so do not even think of challenging me'. He also informed them that he would put something in the newspaper and that is what he did. He put a notice in The Derbyshire Times and mentioned his achievements, where he lived and even where he was to be employed and live with me, but he didn't mention his parents at all, they must have been so hurt.

Our children all gained degrees and I am immensely proud of their achievements and I don't think that I am taking anything away from them by telling other people how proud I am of them. When any of my friend's children achieve something, they share it with their family and friends and I as others like to say 'well done, congratulations' to their child. It is nice to share good things with people that you know.

Chapter Nine

Building our Future

Phil had gained employment with a chemical company on Teesside, so we moved away from our family and friends. We rented a company house for a few months at Wilton which was close to the plant where Phil worked, I began working for Cleveland County Council in Middlesbrough in the Salaries Department, this was in a much larger office environment than I was used to, but I soon made some new friends. We intended to buy a house and even more so as the company house was far too close to the plant and the previous tenants had not looked after the house at all. They had even painted the internal walls in dark green and dark brown and the paintwork was the same, it was quite depressing to return home to each day. George's' sister, Evelyn and her husband Brian had called in to see us on the way back from Newcastle where he had been on a course they took one look at the house and said, 'Can't you buy a house now?' We said that we had been looking and had seen some new ones that were being built in a place called Skelton. All four of us went to look at the new houses, Uncle Brian was impressed with them and asked us why we didn't buy one of them. Phil informed him that we hadn't saved up enough deposit yet. Uncle

Brian said, 'Can't your Dad lend it to you?' after Phil said 'No' Uncle Brian said, 'Go to the bank and ask them to lend the deposit to you'. We did this, we had our first mortgage. We began to buy our first house in the December after we had moved to Teesside. We moved into a brand-new build house, it had been built by Wimpey's it had two double bedrooms and a bathroom upstairs with a living room and kitchen downstairs. We couldn't afford to have central heating or a garage, so we had the heating put in the following year when our finances improved and a garage the following year, but Phil dug out the foundations for the garage as it was cheaper to do it that way.

I had not been baptised as a baby and even though I had gone to Sunday school at the Methodist Church in Maltby as a child no one thought to baptise me. One evening I said to Phil I would like to be baptised, I had been thinking about if for a long time. We decided to go to Church services in Skelton now we were settled. We went to evensong for a while as we didn't think that we would be able to get up in time for the 10am service on Sundays. Then we tried the 10am service as the book used in Evensong was very old to us and no other young people went to that service. At the 10am service we quickly made friends with the Rector, his wife and some of the other younger parishioners. I was baptised on the Easter Sunday with Uncle Brian and Auntie Evelyn as my Sponsors (Godparents). In the summer Phil and I were confirmed together. Although he had attended church as a child and Ann made a big thing about me not being able to receive communion at Midnight Mass on Christmas Eve at the Crooked Spire, but neither could

Phil. We were very much part of the Church community and it became a large part of our social life as we
spent a great deal of time with people who were a part
of the church community, going on walks and visiting
each other's homes in the evenings. We were part of a
group called Worship Workshop where groups of people
across all ages shared and practised different arts such
as music, dance and drama to be included in services. It
was great fun and was lovely for the youngsters to be a
part of the church services in such a prominent way.

Phil and I attended more training courses especially
during lent to find out more about Christianity. We even
hosted groups in our home and Phil began to lead some
of the sessions. A couple that we were particularly
close to lead a marriage enrichment event one weekend
so we both attended that. I wasn't very happy to be told
that I allowed Phil to control me and neither did he, so
we didn't attend any more of these sessions. At that
point I could not see that I was being controlled. We
were a team, best friends as well as husband and wife
and we were looking forward to the future that we were
building. Life was exciting.

When we had discussed having children as you do before
you marry and during the early years of marriage we
had always said that we would have four children and
even bounced names around, what their names would
be. When we decided that we could afford to have
children or with hindsight Phil decided that we could
afford to as he had always managed our household
accounts, we both became worried as I hadn't conceived
after about six months. We visited the GP and we were

referred to a consultant. Then we had a new daily ritual, Phil took and recorded my temperature on a chart each morning before I got out of bed. There were a few occasions that we did pregnancy tests as I was very late having my period the chart was difficult for us to read as my menstrual cycle was all over the place there were quite a few tears shed during that time due to the disappointments. We went through some of the investigative tests and when I did get pregnant we were absolutely delighted, I didn't really believe it even though I was suffering from morning sickness. I still can't bear the thought of eating Weetabix, they really are not nice second time around! We were absolutely delighted to be given the gift of children. Our first child was born on George's' birthday, George was so pleased to be a Grandad for the first time and the baby being born on his birthday. He had joked with me before the baby was born that if the baby was born on his birthday he would buy me some flowers, the baby was due on 13th May but was born on 5th of May. George did buy me flowers, they were delivered to the hospital which made up for the fact that Phil hadn't done so, unlike all the other fathers. In retrospect I think he felt that his nose had been pushed out, everyone's attention was on me and the new-born baby not him. Also, now there was someone else that would take my attention away from him it was a little like when the young man, with Downs Syndrome had put his arm around me. Phil didn't like to share me, he wanted my full attention.

Four years after moving into our house in Skelton we had outgrown it due to having a baby and the equipment they need so we put it on the market and managed to sell it quickly. We managed to find a larger house that we would be able to extend further but it was already much larger than the house that we had. It had a kitchen with a serving hatch to the separate dining room, a large living room, another large room that was used as a bedroom and a bathroom, upstairs there was a large bedroom with the possibility of building further rooms on the back of the house and at the front which is what we eventually did. Meanwhile during the process of selling and buying another house Phil had been offered a two-year secondment in Corpus Christi, Texas, USA. Although as a first time Mum I was worried about leaving everyone I knew, and losing the support they gave me with looking after the baby, Phil persuaded me that it was going to be good for his career and our future, so we seized this opportunity and only lived in our second house for a few weeks before we packed up and left for a new adventure, we would rent the house out fully furnished whilst we were away and we would rent a house in Texas. I was upset to be leaving family and friends but also a little excited and knowing that we would be back after a year for a visit helped enormously, as did knowing that it was for just two years. It was very scary moving to another country without even visiting it, but the company would be supporting us and paying for the move. Corpus Christi is on the Gulf of Mexico, the Gulf is amazing but extremely hot. Within days of arriving and when we were still staying in a hotel I became quite ill, being sick, we did a pregnancy test, but it was negative, we thought it might be due to the heat and the humidity. The sickness however didn't abate and then I began vomiting blood, it was even

difficult to keep water down. We had to quickly register
with a GP and I attended an appointment, we discovered that I was indeed pregnant this was within a week
of arriving in Corpus Christi. The GP; informed me
that if the vomiting didn't stop then I would have to be
admitted to hospital as I would become dehydrated.
The Nurse suggested that I sucked ice chips; small
slivers of ice and to try and eat very small amounts of
food. This was all very scary for me especially as I was
in a strange country and had no family there to help me
and I couldn't even pick up the phone to ask for advice
from my Mum as and when I needed to as there was a
six-hour time difference. We managed to rent a nice
four bedroomed house quickly, but I spent moving day
laid down due to the vomiting, we had purchased most
of the furniture we needed from the couple that were
returning to the UK, and managed to have brief shopping trips to purchase the basics we needed until our air
and sea freight arrived. Fortunately, within a few weeks
the sickness and the nausea ceased so I became fully
mobile again. We also bought a 3.5. litre American car,
a Cutlass Supreme. During our time there we spent
most weekends on the beach and travelled extensively
we packed in quite of lot of during the two years we
lived there. It was very hard not having any family
support for me, in particular looking after two young
children day to day and especially at first when I was
looking after a new-born and a two-year-old. Ann and
George visited us for a few weeks in the December after
we had moved there, staying for Christmas with us.
My Mum and Stepdad also visited a month later, but
they were shocked and very upset as was I when Phil

smacked our 20-month-old for crying and screaming as she wanted me and not my Mum who had taken her from me so that I could eat my meal. We had taken Mum and my Stepdad to Houston to visit the Kennedy Space Centre and to stay over the night before their flight back to the UK. She had become ill with a high temperature during the visit to the Space Centre. I went and sat in the car for a while and gave her some medication to reduce her temperature, but she only wanted to be with me and he found that a problem. We discovered she had an ear infection but as we were out of town we didn't discover that until we returned to Corpus Christi the following day. There were other incidents over the years when Phil had outbursts of temper on one occasion leading to one of our children having their fingers trapped in a car door and having to be taken to hospital. These incidents reminded me of Jack and unnerved me but also made me cross. Shortly after our second child was born my nephew and niece came to stay with us for a few weeks. Which was nice, my niece nicknamed the new baby Peewee after a cartoon character due to him having a quiff of hair on the top of his head. I made some lovely friends both American and British especially at the ceramics classes that I attended, I even completed a course in ceramics from the beginning of the process to the end using different techniques. I also travelled to Dallas to a conference with the owners of the business where I did my classes leaving Phil at home with our two children for a few days. I had an amazing time meeting lots of different people and went to some training seminars to learn and complete some new techniques. We ladies at the conference even went to Labares nightclub one night, it was a male strip show, I found it hilarious all these men cavorting around the stage and striping down to a posing pouch that women put dollars into in exchange for a kiss. I think my Mum would have fainted at the sight of it all. On the last night there was a dinner dance. I was asked to dance several times, but it was American Country dancing, so I declined. One man spent ages talking to me that evening, later Petra told me that she had sent him away. Apparently, he thought he stood a good chance of getting me to spend the night with him. That horrified me I hadn't a clue that was his motive, I thought he was just being friendly. Naïve or what? I was glad to return to the safety of my home in Corpus Christi. Why do married men think it is appropriate to do such things?

When we lived in Corpus Christi Phil became friendly with one of the secretaries and she and her husband visited our house and we visited theirs. I felt most uncomfortable around the husband and didn't like some of the things that they spoke about. I kept quiet or tried to change the subject. It wasn't like that with any of our other friends, there were innuendoes and rude jokes with other friends from time to time but this was on a different plane it frequently became quite explicit. I didn't encourage any further visits I just didn't know how to deal with it. If it was now I would tell them to get out of my house.

Although it had been difficult leaving England for two years it was very sad leaving Corpus Christi and I would have stayed longer as the lifestyle was much better than in the UK due mainly to the warmer climate and being able to spend more time outdoors and visiting different places. The pay was very good too and I could have the car every day as the other British couple there for two years had two cars and if they were away one of Phil's American colleagues gave him a lift to and from work. Although I did ask Phil about getting a second car like the other couples he responded that we didn't need to and that we needed to save money for our return to England, that the house there would need a great deal spending on it. It was also difficult to leave the lovely friends that I had made especially through the ceramics classes that I attended. We decided that we should return to the UK as Phil and I agreed that the children should grow up near their Grandparents and our wider family which due to my childhood having been unstable at times, I wanted our children to have a lovely secure childhood and be part of an extended family as I had experienced when I lived with my Mum and Dad as a child in Maltby. Also, Phil had experienced a childhood surrounded by family we returned home. We moved back into the house that we had only lived in for a few weeks before leaving for the States. It seemed very small compared to the house that we had lived in in Corpus Christi. We decided to remain in Skelton and extend and modernise the house including a new kitchen which we did. We bought a car on our return to the UK, Phil needed it to travel to work and I believed him when he said that we couldn't afford to run two cars. If I needed the car I had to take him to work and then pick him up at the end of the day. As when we lived in Corpus Christi, other people who had the same role in the company had two cars, I could never fully under-stand why we couldn't be the same, but I trusted him with our finances, why shouldn't I? We reacquainted ourselves with the friends that we had before we left the UK and we made some new friends too due to the chil-dren now attending playgroups and the infants school.

We began to attend the same church on our return as that is where our friends went. Phil continued to increase his role in the church and most weeks was either the crucifer or another role.

The year after returning from Texas we discussed whether to have baby number three, we had a two-year-old and a four-year-old and we decided to go ahead. I had been a little reluctant as I was twenty-nine and wanted to go to college and get the qualifications that I had been denied by Jack. I didn't want to get to the point in my life that Ann had when her children left home and she felt that she had nothing to look forward to for herself. She had however learned how to sew and made herself some lovely things after I had encouraged her to go to a night classes. I continued to try and persuade her to drive again but she always remained nervous and George didn't seem to encourage her. Anyway, I became pregnant very quickly. After my problems with initially conceiving I had been advised not to take the contraceptive pill again so I think that solved the fertility issues that I had experienced initially. This time I was nauseous in the early stages of pregnancy but not to the extent of continuous vomiting that I had suffered previously. When I was several months pregnant Phil's behaviour changed. At first, I put it down to Gran Thomas being ill and dying but he began staying out late and going out at nights, he was becoming extremely selfish and repeatedly said that he 'needed time' to himself, he didn't even consider that I might need free time. He didn't see being at home with children and looking after the home as an important role at all. We still had the furniture that we had bought over

11 years ago and the carpets in the house that we had bought before going to Corpus Christi were threadbare in places, but this didn't bother him in the slightest. He even went to a works Christmas Party without me, which he had never done before, he didn't return until the early hours of the morning I was worried sick, I had no way of contacting him. I did ring the venue where the party had been held but everyone had left. When he eventually arrived back home in the early hours of the morning I was very angry and asked him who he had been with and if he was having an affair, he denied it. He informed me that he was going to play badminton at dinner times and so would be off site if I needed him, but his kit was never dirty, I had no way of checking this out as I didn't have access to the car, he had it. Even if I had it would have been difficult as I had to pick our younger child up from nursery and give him his dinner and even if I had gone down to Redcar to check if he was there he would have made an excuse, he was very quick thinking, I knew that he was lying to me. Phil continued to behave strangely towards me but not when our friends or family were present, then everything was normal, he was very good at playing the part of being the happy family man. By the time I was heavily pregnant I confided in a close friend, the Rectors wife that I thought Phil was having an affair. She was shocked and said 'No, he wouldn't,' All she ever saw was Phil in the church or within a small worship group where he would be praying and speaking in tongues. I was adamant that he was and one night when he had gone out again she and other friends tried to find him to no avail, he certainly wasn't where he said he was going to be. My mind was in turmoil, I knew that he was having an

affair, he repeatedly denied it and kept saying that he wouldn't do that, he loved me and the children. He used to also say that he would like to go bird watching, a friend of ours was a keen bird watcher and Phil had been a member of the RSPB since childhood, he would talk to this friend at the end of church or when attending small house groups and he would become excited about the birds the friend had seen. He then began to go either on the Saturday or Sunday afternoon to bird watch by himself. Interestingly, he never went with our friend who had that common interest. He was constantly leaving me at home heavily pregnant with two small children to look after. Looking back, I can only explain that by using a voice that was authoritarian and shocked that I would think such a thing of him made me feel it was me imagining things when he said 'no, I wouldn't do that, I love you'. It was like him saying 'how dare you think I would do such a thing'. I think you would need to go through the same experience to fully understand it.

As we only had the one car at that time and if I needed it then I would have to take him to work and pick him up at the end of the day. On one occasion I was in the car waiting for him outside work and a woman came out of the building accompanied by a man, the woman turned around and smiled or rather smirked at me. There was something in that look that made me feel uneasy it told me that she was the other woman. It was as though she was letting me know. None of the other women did it. I asked Phil about her and he said 'Oh, she is married to a policeman' that was her husband. He knew exactly who I was talking about after I gave him a very brief description, I felt sick. He was still denying that he was having an affair and by saying that was her husband he was attempting to tell me it wasn't her.

A few weeks later when I was about 36 weeks pregnant, we went to an Italian restaurant in Redcar for our joint birthday meal, one of the waiters looked across at us strangely several times and whispered something to his colleague who then looked at us. When the waiter was serving us, he said to Phil 'You have been here before haven't you sir, I served you?' Phil said that he hadn't, I could tell that he was lying. The look in the waiter's eyes said it all, he had served Phil before and he was denying it to the waiter because he had been with someone else. The waiter looked at me with a pitying expression, later when I returned from the ladies' toilet, he could obviously see that I was heavily pregnant, he also said something to his colleague who again looked our way and shook his head. My suspicion of course grew further the waiter had recognised Phil, what is more he knew Phil had been with a different woman to his heavily pregnant wife. I felt so sick, I still couldn't prove anything and a part of me was also afraid of the truth. We had two small children and I was carrying another baby, what was I going to do? Over the final weeks of my pregnancy I lost a great deal of weight through all the worry and stress, Phil was still denying it and patronising me, my mind was all over the place, I felt like I was going mad, what was I going to do? The midwife and the GP, who was also a friend asked me several times why I was losing weight I said that I didn't know, I couldn't say 'I think my husband is having an affair and I am worried about my children and the baby that I am carrying. At the time I thought that I was losing my mind. Our friends were also saying 'no, he wouldn't do that'. They saw him as the perfect husband, father and Christian man who prayed with them in small prayer groups and carried the big cross in the church, read the bible readings and said the prayers in church that he had so eloquently written.

Phil didn't change his selfish behaviour and on the Sunday night that I went into labour Phil had been out until late and went off to bed as soon as he got in, the poor man was tired. I informed him that I was in labour, he didn't show any concern or excitement or offer to sit up with me, he said he was going to bed, I said that I would wake him up if I needed him. I walked around downstairs for hours rubbing my own back. At 3 am I woke him up and said that I needed to go to hospital. He got up and our friends came to look after our two children, we met our GP friend at the local hospital. As the baby was being born I said to Phil 'Look, look at your baby'. He looked at his son entering the world, you wouldn't think that he was having an affair with another woman, he was very happy having a new son. I only stayed in the hospital until teatime, I was worried sick all day I had such irrational thought such as he would move the other woman into our house if I wasn't there. That was the state of my mind by then, no one was believing that Phil was having an affair. My Mum and Stepdad came to visit and meet the new baby and she asked me what was wrong, she thought that I looked ill and stressed. I broke down in tears and told her that Phil was having an affair and why I thought he was but that he was denying it. They were very shocked as they had treat him like a son, and they also didn't think that he would do such a horrible thing to me. They challenged Phil, but he denied it to their faces as well I felt so alone and stressed. A few days later, Phil went out again, he had said that he 'needed a break' as he had been at home all week. So, he left me alone with a 5-day old baby, a very active into everything two-year-old and a four-year-old all afternoon. I was living with this torment going through my mind every minute of the day and night, trying to feed and look after our new born baby and the other two children. While Phil was out I finally managed to contact one of his work colleagues and I asked him if Phil was having an affair and did he know her name. I felt that I needed her name, so that I could challenge Phil. The friend replied that he had suspected that Phil was having an affair, Phil had denied it to him. He informed me what her name was I was, absolutely devastated. When Phil returned home from having 'my time,' I challenged him I said to him firmly, 'You are having an affair, and said her name. His face was a picture he was so shocked that he appeared to find it difficult to speak. After all these months of denying it and making me feel so stressed and in my opinion putting our unborn baby at risk I was furious I shouted at him to choose between her or me and not to even think about staying with me for the children, to leave them out of it. He then said 'You, I choose you, I love you'. I then told him to ring her, he said that he would tell her on the Monday. I said 'No, you will ring her here and now in front of me'. He picked up the phone dialled her number and told her that I had found out and that it was over between them. Within less than half an hour she was knocking on our door. The cheek of it, she lived in Redcar and we lived in Skelton, she had obviously been to our home at some point to get there so quickly as Medway Close was quite difficult to find, we didn't have sat navs then. Phil had the audacity to invite her in, he even asked her if she wanted some dinner and a drink, I so felt like hitting her and him but was far too weak and tired and stunned that she had the audacity to come to our home. I had lost loads of weight with the worry and stress, given birth to a baby five days ago and had been looking after all three children all day whilst he had been having fun with her. They didn't seem to consider any of this at all. I didn't want her anywhere near my baby either. She sat in the living room with our tatty settee, the one we had bought 12 years previously, threadbare carpet and a room that was in much need of being decorated but my husband had been far too busy with her to do what he should have been doing at the home where he lived with his wife and children. We didn't have money to decorate and replace furniture, we had money to fund him going to Italian restaurants and wherever with her. Phil again told her it was over, he also cried as well and said that he had loved us both! Really? That hurt me further but now I think; how pathetic, what he had loved was pretending to be a family man and being a free and single man for months. He felt so sorry for himself or sorry that he had been caught out that is why he cried, anyway hadn't he told me that crying was emotional blackmail? I also made him ring my Mum and tell her that he had been having an affair and that he had lied to her. I also informed the friends that had tried to help me before I had the baby that he had been having an affair, he had made me feel like I was going mad. When I went for my post-natal check our GP friend who had been so worried about my weight loss before the baby's birth said 'well, do you have something to tell me?' One of our friends had informed her about what had happened as they had all been so worried about me and the baby. I broke down and told her everything. She then put me on anti-depressants and tried to reassure me that they wouldn't hurt the baby. I took them for a few days and then flushed them down the toilet I didn't trust taking medication when I was breast feeding and wanted the best for my baby. I was also determined that I wouldn't allow him, and the 'other woman' make me ill, they had already of course but my mind was still all over the place and I thought talking anti-depressants meant they had achieved something more to what they had already achieved. They obviously worked at the same place which was extremely difficult for me as much of their affair had been conducted at work. During dinner times he admitted that they had gone to her Mums house and when he was supposed to be bird spotting. Her mother was living in Saudi with her husband and a younger daughter, it was all very convenient for them as she had a door key to her mother's house, they had a perfect hideaway.

The following months were difficult I remained very stressed and worried, I was trying to cope with a baby a three year old and a five year old, clean, cook and all the other chores. Phil continued to feel sorry for himself I think due to other people knowing the horrendous thing that he had done, he had fallen off his pedestal. On one occasion after I had rung work he wasn't there, no one could find him. I wrote down my feelings about what had happened over the last few months and how difficult it was to cope with. Phil wrote me a letter to reinforce what he was saying to me that was almost three pages in length. Although I have ownership of the letter I am not allowed to publish it but can quote what he said to me and portions of the letter. He promised me that he wouldn't say anything that he didn't mean. He said, *'it makes me feel sick with guilt and remorse, I certainly loved you throughout (I have always loved you) and I know now that I did not feel love for her'*. He went on to say that *'I think I was in love with the excitement, but it wasn't excitement – I hated it throughout'*. He blamed Satan; *'I could feel Satan getting hold of my life, I just couldn't stop it. I hadn't prayed enough but am healed now.'* He promised that he wouldn't do it again as he was safe. He stated that he *'didn't want to belittle'* everything we had done together over the last 15 years, that they were just as important to him as me. That he *'wanted every child we had .'* He continued by saying *' I want you to put your trust in me, but I recognise that will take time'*. He promised me that he would *'never hide anything'* from me again. He also said; *' I am praying for you'* and that he wanted me to know that he loved me with all his heart. Phil continued to say the things that you would expect a person who didn't want to break a marriage up to say, maybe even like those men and women who commit domestic abuse say, that he had never been happier as he knew now how wonderful life with me had been and that he wanted to share the rest of his life with me. He realised how close he had come to losing me. How was I supposed to respond to that? He came across as a desperate man who had truly learnt his lesson, I was very vulnerable and not as strong as I am now. In reality, nothing could ever justify or excuse his behaviour. Any man or woman who thinks it is okay to put a pregnant woman through what he put me through are selfish, self-centred and arrogant. At the time I blamed myself I thought that it because I was fat (pregnant), he had gone off me, all the irrational thoughts that go through your mind when you have been put into that situation. He never took any responsibility for his behaviour; his conscience didn't allow him to admit it was totally his choice to do what he had done. It didn't put her in a good light either. By saying that everything we had done over the past 15 years (that was from being 15 years old) were as important to him as me was supposed to reassure me. Also, that he was praying for me as though that was supposed to make me feel better, that he had my best interests at heart. My Mum and Albert had invited me and the children to move in with them, but I decided to work through this horrendous situation as I truly believed at the time that he had learnt a lesson and it was the right thing to do as a Christian, support him and help him recover from his experience of Satan. Now when I think about it. It was using religion as a form of control over me.

I met with the other woman on several occasions following the visit that she had made to our home on that Saturday night. She came to visit me at home. I wanted to know why when she who had only been married for a couple of years thought it was acceptable to have an affair with a married man whose wife was pregnant with their third child. Amongst other things she informed me that her Mum and Dad had divorced and how that had hurt her so much and how she wished her Mum and Dad had not split up. What she said was so bizarre, the hurt she had felt when her own parents had split up had not been enough to stop her from doing it to two small children and an unborn child. When I asked her again why she had done it when she knew it would hurt my children her reply was 'I wanted your life'. So, this selfish vile woman thought she could just step into my shoes and take over my life. Not only that she was prepared to be with a man who had affairs when his wife was pregnant! What right minded woman would want to even think of doing that? Phil informed me that she had told her husband about the affair and that he had hit her causing bruising to her face. About a year later she had a baby herself, Phil after I asked him said that it wasn't his baby it was her husbands.

It was all very difficult to try and rebuild trust with Phil I didn't want him to go out and about which was irrational in some ways as his affair with the woman had been at their workplace. I do have another note he wrote me swearing his undying love but won't bore you with it as it is pretty much in the same vein as the other letter he gave me and cards over the following years. He did however decide we did have money to purchase new settees, carpets, curtains and redecorate the house!

Phil rang my Mum and Albert to inform them that he had lied to them and that he had been having an affair. They were furious with him and insisted that Ann and George were informed and that if I didn't inform them then they would. After Ann and George had been informed they visited us for the day but Phil was at work, he didn't want to face his parents. Ann informed me 'Sarah says that this is all Phil's fault, but I don't, I blame you, it's your fault, our Phil needs lots of love and attention and you give the children far too much attention'. She said this just after I had been prescribed anti-depressants by the GP. I was also at that time holding her newly born Grandchild in my arms that I was breastfeeding, getting up several times during the night to do that whilst her son slept soundly. He always said that he had not heard the baby wake up. Her other two Grandchildren were running around as children do, she could not consider that Phil was in the wrong. George was stood there and said nothing, he just looked away exasperated with her. He didn't defend her, but he didn't defend me either. After my Mum had the affair with Albert, Ann had stopped speaking to her and always tried to ignore my Mum. After Ann passed away my Mum despite having dementia, said 'she didn't like me you know, she used to ignore me' at family events she would completely snub my Mum. She always said how she was disgusted with this person or that person if they had had affairs but when it came to Phil having one it wasn't his fault at all. When I informed Phil what she had said, he gave the usual response of 'ignore her, she isn't very bright, I will have a word with her'. He also told me that I was a good wife and mother when I asked 'what am I supposed to do? Not look after the children's needs? Years later I informed all my children that if they have an affair then I will stick up for their spouse and if there are children involved then I will support the spouse even more and disown them. If you are not happy within your marriage do the decent thing and leave in a civilised way and make sure you pay for your responsibilities. Do not bring a third person in to make yourself feel good as it isn't good at all. It is selfish, spiteful and hateful.

Things settled down but two years later Phil and I lost our fourth child. I had gone for a scan, but the baby had died. I was induced and gave birth to a son at 11.30pm who we named Jonathan. Jonathan was cremated but only Phil and I went to the funeral, he didn't want either set of Grandparents there and I was still in shock and too distraught to argue that I really wanted my Mum there. If you have been through that experience you will know that you never get over it, you learn to live with it. I still grieve for the baby I lost and have a rose bush in my garden that I call the 'Jonathan rose'. Interestingly enough though, Phil insisted that we went on the caravan holiday to Caernarvon that had been booked and paid for a few months before we lost Jonathan. I really wanted to stay at home to recover from what I had been through. Phil however insisted that we went on the holiday. While we were there I started losing clots of blood and had to go to hospital to get checked out. I was told to take it easy but there was no chance of that and we did lots of walking. On the way back home from Wales we stopped at Ann and George's in Chesterfield, the baby wasn't mentioned at all by anyone, it was as though none of it had happened. We didn't call in to see my Mum who hadn't seen me since I had given birth to Jonathan we went straight home from Ann and George's'. We had always shared our time equally between all Grandparent's as that was fair to them and the children, so it was strange not to visit my Mum or Dad too but as always Phil was in charge.

I had started studying with the Open University but didn't recommence the course after losing Jonathan. My heart wasn't in it and Phil said that the stress of doing it had probably contributed towards Jonathan dying. When I think about that now I think how dared he say that to me. Especially after the stress that he had put me under when I was pregnant with our third child. But then how dared he keep my Mum away from me when I was in such a state grieving for my baby? How dared he make me go away on a holiday when all I wanted to do was curl up in a ball in my own place of safety, my home?

A year later our fifth baby was born so we had the four children that we had always said we would have. The four of them have been my biggest and the best achievement of my life. I am very proud of them all. By delaying my own education and building a career for myself, I was able to be a stay at home mum and did so until the youngest child was two years old. Each of my children were taught by me how to feed themselves, dress themselves, use the toilet including wiping their bottoms clean, how to wash themselves, clean their teeth and wash their hair properly, read, write, draw, do arts and crafts. They made Christmas cards and calendars for family and friends with lots of cotton wool and glitter stuck on them at Christmas. They were always bought books to read, I also took them to the library, they all love reading as I do as I encouraged them to develop that knowledge of the gift and being able to read. When they were small I spend most of my time on the floor and always had hard skin on my knees and the top of my feet due to crawling around the floor playing with them building things, playing with shape sorters and jigsaws. Phil did say to me once that when the children were older very young that once they were he would stay at home and I could go to work instead of him. He thought I was having it far too easy being at home with four children. As the children got older I taught them how to wash, iron and cook meals. They are all bright and look out for each other although there can still be some name calling and tormenting even though they are supposed to be grown up. All four of our children did very well at school and continued with their education by going to University after college. Maybe I drummed it into them that it was easier to get a degree straight from school rather than as adults when you have so many other things to juggle. They all have degrees and three of them have higher degrees too. One is a civil servant, one is a Vicar, one is a Doctor and the youngest is currently living and working in Sydney, Australia and doing very well for herself.

Chapter Ten

A Stepmum

My Dad rang me out of the blue one night, he very rarely rang so it was quite a surprise. He was very excited as he told me he was getting married in a couple of days' time. Married! I didn't even know he was even seeing anyone, he had been by himself for just over twelve years. He informed me that he had met her two weeks ago! Her daughter was the manager of the betting shop and Joyce helped out. He told me how wonderful the lady was and that they were going to live at his house after they married. The lady, Joyce was living with her son at that moment as she had sold her flat. I said I would come down the night before the wedding and meet Joyce and would stay at my Mums. Phil said that he couldn't take time off work at such short notice, so I drove down the night before the wedding with the two children and stayed at Mums. Mum looked after the children and put them to bed while I went to meet Joyce for the first time. It was around this time that Phil's behaviour changed and when maybe the woman he had the affair with had visited our house.

I drove around to my Dads and then took him to where Joyce was staying and met her, one of her sons and his family. Joyce it turned out had had been married to my Mum's ex fiancés brother. My Dad started talking about my Mum and even made some negative comments about my Mums past that I did not like at all. When Mum was younger she had gone into the Queens Hotel, a pub in Maltby with her Dad and he had bought her a drink of port and lemon, Mum was meeting someone else a little later but had enough time to have a drink with her Dad. Anyway, a young man who was in the Queens offered to escort Mum to where she was going, Grandad was happy with this but the man sexually assaulted her, the case went to court but because Mum had been in the pub and had the drink of port and lemon they threw it out of court the man got away with the assault, Mum was obviously distraught, and her reputation was in tatters. Mum and her fiancé split up over the incident. There was obviously gossip about it, but my Dad was relating the bad side of this not only in front of me, but also in front of Joyce, her son and his partner. My Dad had seen this man at a party at a friend's house close to where we lived when I was in my teens and my Dad had thumped him for what he had done to my Mum all those years ago. We left Joyce's sons shortly afterwards. As I drove my Dad home he was singing Joyce's praises, when I dropped him off at his house he said to me 'what do you think of Joyce'. I was very cross with him and I turned to him but very calmly told him to tell Joyce, that if he said anything bad about my Mum again I would be annoyed. I asked him if Mum and Grandad knew the man and trusted that he would look after her and make sure that she arrived safely where she was going to? He said 'yes'. I asked if Mum would have had too much to drink, he said 'no', she had had one port and lemon. Mum never drank I used to torment her about it loads. I told my Dad again 'tell Joyce my Mum is an amazing lady and she is just that a lady and you know that'. My Dad never said another bad thing about my Mum in front of me and Joyce again, although Joyce occasionally said how Dad had been left all alone and hadn't been looking after himself properly. If he hadn't had an affair in the first place maybe Mum wouldn't have left him or had an affair herself.

Joyce however I discovered very quickly was an amazing lady, she was very family orientated, she had kept her family by working hard all her life, her first husband had let her down a great deal. If any of her children needed support, she was there offering advice and a shoulder to cry on. My Dad was very happy, he had grown up at last I think. He didn't gamble and doted on Joyce as she did him. Joyce would tell him off if I had told him off for saying a swear word in front of my children and he said, 'I haven't sworn', Joyce would back me up and say 'Clarry you have, stop swearing in front of the kiddies'. I think my children loved this banter, Grandad being told off by Mum and Grandma. Joyce was a lovely Stepmum and also a fabulous Grandma to my children. Joyce treat my children the same as her own Grandchildren.   At Christmas for instance she would have huge sacks that she filled with sweets, chocolate, biscuits and all the 'e' numbers she could find. My children and her own Grandchildren were given one of these sacks full of goodies per family unit to share. The children absolutely loved it, they shared it all out and exchanged the ones they didn't like between each other for something they did. She once bought my youngest daughter, Hannah a doll and Hannah called it Tomato. Every single doll that Hannah had, was called Emma apart from Tomato. Joyce was also a fabulous knitter and she knitted all my children Aran jumpers and cardigans. Joyce looked after my Dad very well and when he was in hospital she would arrive there in the morning and stay with him until the end of the day which was very good as Dad had macular degeneration of the eyes and could not see very well at all. Joyce made sure he ate all his meals and drank. She was a lovely generous lady and I was really upset after she died.

Joyce made my Dad very happy and that was the main thing. I still miss speaking to her.

Chapter Eleven

Finally, An Education

Following Phil's affair, one of our friends offered to look after the baby and collect the other two children from school so that I could go to college to begin to get some qualifications for myself and then be able to have a career instead of returning to office work. If you recall I had left school two days after my sixteenth birthday so didn't complete my education. I had managed to do a correspondence course and gained an 'O' level in English when I was pregnant with our first child but hadn't taken any other formal exams.

It was nerve racking returning to the classroom, but I absolutely loved it. I had always read the newspapers and read books, this was a whole new world I attended a local college one afternoon a week studying GCSE Sociology and passed it. The following year I began studying for a degree with the Open University but as I have already informed you I lost the baby I was expecting and was persuaded to take a break. The year after having our youngest child I studied GCSE Maths by attending night classes at a local college and GCE 'A' Level Sociology one afternoon a week with the youngest children being looked after by a childminder, I was able to make it back to Skelton where we were still living to collect the older two children from school. Phil had been promoted and so he had a company car now, so I could finally have the family car, this made my life so much easier. Studying for an 'A' level was brilliant, I had decided to gain enough qualifications so that I could go to university full time when the children were a little older and more independent. I applied for a full time university degree after the college tutor said to me 'Iris, apply for university they will love you, you don't need to get anymore A levels, you can study, you have proven that'. I was offered places to study for all three of the different degrees that I had applied for; Humanities; Law and Social Science. I chose Humanities as it would allow me to study different subjects and then choose a main degree specialism if I preferred to study in more depth one of more of the subjects. It was amazing going to university full time. Organising childcare was fairly stressful, I managed to get a student loan to pay for childcare and the books that I would need to buy. We had by this time moved from Skelton to the outskirts of Middlesbrough so that was much easier to get to the University of Teesside every day. We had outgrown the house in Skelton after having our youngest daughter and decided it would also be of benefit to ourselves and any neighbours that we lived in a detached property, potentially we could have four teenagers playing differ-ent kinds of music in their rooms. The youngest child, Hannah attended the university nursery which made it easier for me to get her there each morning, collect her after lectures and be in time for collecting the older children from school. The university were very support-ive of mature students with children and our timetables meant that we were placed in lectures and seminars that enabled us to get away by three o clock each day so that we could also get to collect the children from school in time, I could do the journey in under half an hour if the traffic wasn't too busy. We often had timetables with no breaks and our study time would be completed at home. The children even accompanied me to lectures during the half term holidays as did other student's children.

It was quite nerve racking preparing for University especially after I had purchased some of the books off the reading list and flipped through them and read little sections of each one. I worried that I wouldn't be able to cope with it and having to write essays that would be marked. My first year at University however was fantastic I soaked it all up, German, Politics, Drama and Poetry, History and History of Ideas. The other students including the younger ones were also nervous when they handed in the first essays and they had come straight from school to university so were used to writing essays and sitting exams. At the end of the first year I chose to study for an honours degree in History, although I enjoyed the other subjects Social History had become my favourite subject.

One of my student friends asked me if I wanted to go to the student's union one night and out of curiosity I said that I would, Phil agreed that I could go and said that he would look after the children and he even drove me down to the university. It was very dark and noisy like a disco with youngsters drinking massive quantities of alcohol. The student that I had gone with was another 'mature student' but unmarried and didn't have any children, we were to share a taxi at 11pm so I would be home well before 11.30. My friend got talking to someone else and then decided to go on somewhere else. I queued for a taxi by myself and arrived home half an hour later than expected, we didn't have mobile phones then, so I was unable to call and say I was going to be late. The reception I received was not what I expected, Phil was like an angry parent 'What time do you call this? Where have you been? Who have you been with?' He was accusing me of what he had done, I was furious, how dare he. I told him what had happened and went to bed, the next day he said that he was worried that I would have an affair. I said that I would not do that ever. His reply was 'well I did it to you'. His affair had been five years previously. I then shouted at him 'I would never ever do that because I know what it feels like to be cheated on and I would never do that to anyone.' What I also meant was that I would not do that as it would also hurt my children and my family and friends. I didn't want anyone to think I was the kind of woman that slept around with other men. Girls that have been in care are supposed to be promiscuous and have at least five children by the time that are 19 to different men. I had been faithful in my marriage, I strongly believed (and still do) in fidelity and had no intention of breaking that trust. I firmly believed that if I had slept around or committed adultery then I would be betraying all that my Mum had taught me about being a good person, even though she herself had had an affair. Phil also occasionally said that other men fancied me in an accusing way and got very angry and sulked about it. He did not like it at all if I spoke to another man and if I laughed during a conversation he was even more annoyed with me later, but it was okay for him to speak to other women again bizarre behaviour. Don't get me wrong I do see a man and maybe think he's nice looking but really, I have not and would not be interested in ever going down that route. I prefer the security of being in a monogamous relationship with a likeminded person and would never lower my moral standards.

During the time that I was at university due to having four children ten years and younger I always tried to keep ahead in my studies and during the inter semester breaks I worked full days on my studies as well as cleaning the house and looking after the children when they came in from school. During half terms I often took all four of them to lectures. The lecturers were great about it and my children had bags with activities such as reading and drawing in to occupy them, my eldest son appeared to really enjoy listening to the lectures. During the long summer break between my second and third year before the children broke up for their summer holidays I worked every week day on my dissertation so that I would be ahead for what was going to be a very busy year, my dissertation was well on the way to being completed apart from statistics that I needed to research at Church House in London and York.

During late August and through September I began to feel unwell, very tired and had pains in my right hip and knee. Despite visiting the doctor's surgery several times, and having to call out doctors during the night. One of the on-call doctors even suggested that I sat in a bath of warm water at 3am one morning, they were unable to diagnose me. The pains gradually got worse and I remember feeling so exhausted, ill and in so much pain I returned to see a doctor again as small bruises had also appeared on my legs, I thought that they might be due to some medication that he had prescribed me. He informed me to make an appointment to see the nurse the next morning for a blood test. They also made me a follow up appointment with the GP that afternoon. When I arrived in his surgery he looked a little agitated, he wheeled himself over to me on his chair the GP informed me that I had leukaemia he was very upset and when I asked him if I was going to die he said that he didn't know.

I was in total shock, it felt like being hit hard with an invisible door, my mind was racing all over the place, what would happen to the children if I died? Would I die? I had never heard of anyone surviving leukaemia, one of our friend's daughters was currently fighting it. The GP asked if anyone was with me I informed him that Phil had gone to collect the children from school and was returning to collect me as I felt too weak to drive. He rang through to reception and asked them to send Phil in as soon as he arrived. He informed Phil when he arrived at the surgery to collect me. I couldn't tell Phil myself and I didn't know what to say, I had a huge lump in my throat and my eyes were prickling with tears. If I had tried to speak I thought I would burst. Phil took control and asked what was to happen. The GP said that everything was arranged that I had to go into hospital the following morning and that we would find out more then. We went home and ordered pizzas for the children, we decided not to say anything to them at that point as we couldn't answer any questions. Very close family and a couple of very close friends were told that night.

When we arrived at the General Hospital in Middlesbrough the following morning we met with the Doctor who was to be my consultant and some other members of the team. My mind was still all over the place as they explained what would happen. I was put into a room of my own to protect me from infections. Over the next two days I had blood tests and platelet transfusions, my blood had stopped clotting and that is why I had started getting 10p sized bruises on my legs. They informed us that I needed to go to theatre but that wasn't possible until my blood was able to clot. On the Friday I was taken to theatre and had a Hickman line fitted (this would be where all blood tests and transfusions would be done through rather than having to have a cannular fitted. It is a narrow tube that in my case was my inserted into a vein in the neck and was tunnelled under my skin with the end of the line coming out between my breasts and secured onto my chest. A Hickman line allows chemotherapy, bloods, platelets, antibiotics etc to be given directly into the bloodstream. The nurses also took the daily blood tests through the Hickman line as constantly sticking needles into your veins causes your veins to collapse. The line can stay in place for weeks or months. Where the Hickman Line comes out of the body, it must be kept very clean as that is where infections can occur. Initially I had one line fitted but patients can have 2 or 3 lines leading off a junction from where the single line leaves the body. A bone marrow test was also carried out when I was in theatre so that they could find out exactly the type of leukaemia that I had and which treatment I would be given. I was diagnosed with Acute Myeloid Leukaemia. Now the battle could commence in earnest.

Although I was extremely ill I believed that I had a choice to make, I could either sink into a deep depression and feel sorry for myself or fight it, I decided that I would try and finish my degree. I thought it would give me a focus other than being Iris the cancer patient, I could continue to be Iris the student. In no way am I saying that I was positive all the time or not frightened about the possible outcome and I wasn't happy and jolly all the time either. For me, by keeping my mind busy would stop me thinking about the treatment 24/7. Even though I felt so ill and weak it was boring being in bed most of the time and it seemed that everyone that visited wanted to talk about the treatment, how I was, how I looked and what was going to happen. My dissertation tutor visited me in hospital he informed me how upset everyone was and that lectures had been cancelled after my illness had been announced. We then discussed the work I had already completed and how I would be able to complete it, I would need to change the plan, it had originally been dependent on gathering data from historical records, this was now out of the question as I would be open to catching bugs looking through old documents and being in a public library was no longer feasibl. I would be able to adapt my dissertation. The other modules that I would be taking that year fortunately were mainly going to be assessed by essays rather than exams. Lectures were to be taped for me and I was able to write essays in hospital. One of

Phil's secretaries kindly offered to type up my dissertation for me. This kept me very busy and focussed on something else, some of the doctors took great interest in my reading materials, one even said that he wished that he had studied history instead of medicine! One friend, a fellow student from the university visited me and cried the whole time that she was there. I informed the nurses to never ever allow her in my room again, they didn't. Another student sent me a letter saying how tragic it was. I sent her one back saying, no, it's not tragic, it's tragic if I die and as I haven't been informed that I am going to die I don't want you to tell me that I am. Honestly why do people do this. I felt bad enough as it was without all the morbidity.

A few days after being admitted to hospital I was introduced to the 'Wig lady' apparently, I was going to lose my hair. I didn't believe this at all but chose a wig, I tried on all sorts of wigs including a long blonde curly one. Eventually I chose a nice simple brown bob. After a week of treatment, I discovered quite a lot of my hair on the pillow in the morning after I had woken up, then when I washed my hair in the shower it came off my head in huge clumps. I sat on the floor in the shower and cried, it was true I really had leukaemia my hair was nearly all gone, and I realised that I might even die, now that was scary. It was blooming cold without any hair, wearing the wig helped and a hat when the weather was cold. After being in hospital for a few weeks I was asked by the other consultant if I had any siblings as I may need a bone marrow transplant. I had heard of this but didn't really understand what it was and certainly never expected that I might need one myself. After my first round of chemotherapy was completed another bone marrow test was carried out on me. It was a great relief when the results revealed that I was in remission. I was able to be at home for a few weeks to recover from the first round of chemotherapy but was then was back in hospital for my second round. The journey home at the end of the first round of treatment was very strange, I felt very panicky as soon as we walked out of the hospital and this didn't change in the car, I held on to the side of my seat and felt as though the car was going too fast, It wasn't of course. I think it was a combination of being in hospital for weeks and going home knowing that I had to look after the Hickman Line, take my temperature three times a day and there not being any nurses at hand although we did have the telephone number of the ward if there were any problems especially any rise in my temperature.

The other consultant spoke to me again about having a bone marrow transplant and asked me if I thought my siblings would come and be tested. This concerned me, I asked him many detailed questions that maybe I should or should not have asked. I wanted to know why I might need it and he told me that the odds of me remaining well without a bone marrow transplant were 20%. That was a huge shock, I asked him more questions but later after I had thought about it all and a nurse came in she asked me how I was I broke down in tears, I was terrified. The doctor who was on call came to see me and talked through everything and said that I was responding well to treatment. Even though her words had comforted me I was still very scared, this was extremely serious.

Two more successive treatments were done, I had lost a great deal of weight of course due to being sick and my bowels reacting to the treatment. Most days I saw my children but sometimes I didn't see them as I thought they would be frightened seeing me so ill. They couldn't visit me if they were ill either as my immune system was very low. I continued to go home for short periods of time between treatments, but I think it was very confusing for the children. The nurses even fitted a Hickman line like mine to my youngest child Hannah's doll as she was only four they thought it would help her to not be afraid of the one that I had fitted. In fact, she used to clean her dolls line and then helped me clean mine and redress it when I was at home. At Christmas I was allowed home on Christmas Eve afternoon, but I was so ill I had to go back into hospital on Boxing Day. They had tried to timetable my treatments so that I could be at home for Christmas with my children. Of course, no one knew if that would be my last Christmas, so it was very important to us all that I was home for Christmas. Since moving from Skelton, we attended the Parish Church were we now lived. As Phil was training to be a Lay Reader many of the congregation knew us. A close friend who was a retired nurse put a rota up in the Church asking for help for our family following a notice given during the church services on the Sunday following my diagnosis. People were fantastic, they signed up and did babysitting, ironing etc. My Mum and Stepdad stayed at our house every other week to help Phil with the house and our children, things were ticking over at home and the children were being cared for extremely well. It was one less thing for me to worry about, but it was horrendous being away from my home and children for such long periods of time. Ann, Phil's mother only stayed once for a week, she was too busy during the week looking after Sarah's son.

There were some strange moments when I was in hospital like an elderly gentleman who had some form of dementia walking into my room and peeing all over the floor. During the middle of one night when I had gone to the bathroom I heard a squeaky noise from what appeared to be a trolley the squeaky noise stopped and then there was a thud. I flushed the toilet and washed my hands and as I was opening the door someone pulled it shut and said, 'stay in there'. It was the porters collecting someone who had died. If I heard the noise again it would send a shiver down my spine and I called it the 'death wagon'.

In the February after my fourth and final round of treatment, I became very ill and had to choose whether to have injections to bring my white cells back or not as I was not able to fight a virus that I had contracted. The injections to bring back the white cells could however also bring back the leukaemia cells. I asked my consultant what he would do, he replied that he wasn't allowed to tell me and that I had to decide. It was due to this honesty the Doctors had that I had confidence in them and believed that I could trust them. I had the injections but was obviously was very nervous about it for quite a long time. So, there were quite a few scary moments during my initial treatment. My body however began to make white cells I recovered from the virus and when I was well enough I went home to recover in preparation for a potential bone marrow transplant.

During the latter part of my initial treatment, some of my siblings; John; Ken; Robert and Irene were tested to see if they could be bone marrow donors for me. They all had to have a blood test initially. It was good news my two eldest brothers John and Ken both matched. Irene said 'well that's good we always thought you were someone else's' she wasn't joking about this. Blood is amazing Robert had the same blood group as me but didn't match as a bone marrow donor. Further tests had to be done on John, Ken and myself we had to go to the RVI (Royal Victoria Infirmary) in Newcastle for these. This is where the bone marrow transplant would take place. Each of us also had to go through an interview with the transplant team. As part of the process our ability to cope mentally with the transplant was also assessed. John informed me later that he had informed them that if he and Ken were the same level of match then to use him as he would be able to cope better if I died. I said 'charming', but he was probably right. They didn't hide anything from us, if we asked a question it was answered. They informed me that I had a 50% chance of the leukaemia returning without a transplant and a 60% chance of surviving the transplant therefore I didn't feel that I had a choice, the transplant was my best chance long term if the transplant didn't kill me.

During the time that I was recovering and preparing for the transplant, as I became fitter I decided to take the children with me to the local supermarket, this would take some of the pressure from Phil and the children could push the trolley if it got heavy. When we were walking down one of the aisles my eldest child said 'Mum, could you die having this bone marrow transplant', she was almost thirteen years old. What a question to answer in the middle of a supermarket. I said we would discuss it later and when I discussed it with her later I answered her truthfully, 'Yes, I might but hopefully I wouldn't, the doctors are going to make sure that I don't'. You don't lie to anyone but certainly not your own children as they will never trust you again.

Also, during this time my friends twelve-year-old daughter who had been diagnosed with leukaemia six months before me passed away. Phil and I had visited her in the RVI just a few days before she lost her fight, we had been there for me to have further tests done; the removal of some of my flesh that would be put into test tubes and mixed with John's blood to test how much graft versus host I could get so the transplant team would be prepared for what lay ahead.

If anyone has been admitted for this kind of treatment or any kind of cancer treatment you will understand that you really don't know whether you will see another Christmas, your children growing up or on leaving home to commence treatment your home and belongings again. It was terrifying. I always tried to keep my fear hidden from my children and family and think I did a good job of trying to remain positive most of the time. I did of course cry and tell Phil that I was frightened, he always responded that everything would be fine. The process for my bone marrow was to begin on a Friday in May. A few days before we had attended Angela's funeral, I felt so guilty that she had passed away at such a young age, I was being given a chance that she never had. Her family of course didn't feel that way and wanted me to win my fight. Phil and I set off early so that we could go to our favourite Mexican restaurant at the Metro Centre on our way to the RVI. I already knew that I wouldn't be allowed to eat following the transplant, it had been explained to me that my stomach lining and food pipe would be raw from the radiation treatment, I would be drip fed for quite a while and had even been fitted with a double Hickman line that would enable more drugs and other items to be put into my body at the same time. We thought it best to have a lovely meal before I commenced my treatment but were probably both wondering if this would be our last meal out together, at that time I believed that we were fighting this together.

On arriving at the Royal Victoria Infirmary, a bone marrow test was done first to determine if I was still in remission, once this was confirmed I was connected to a drip and given a small bag of chemotherapy. A wow moment was when I was informed that this small bag of chemotherapy was ten times the strength of all the chemotherapy that I had already received. Once the chemotherapy had been given to me I was transferred by ambulance to the General Hospital in Newcastle for TBI (Total Body Irradiation), after three days I returned to the RVI. John was in theatre as I was being transferred to the RVI having his bone marrow removed and when he came around he visited me I was receiving the first bag of his bone marrow. He stayed in overnight and then returned home to Mansfield. I received the final bag of John's bone marrow on the 18th May six years to the day that Jonathan had been born.

Treatment for leukaemia has continually improved as it had over the years by the time I received my treatment.

It wasn't pleasant, there were a few times when I was very ill and couldn't see my children, and when I was in Newcastle I could only see them at the weekend as it was an hour's drive from home and that was far too much for them during the week after school and we wanted them to still continue in their routines such as after school activities they attended, by this time I had my own mobile phone as there was a risk of getting infections from using a public phone, this meant that I could speak to them but it isn't the same as seeing them daily and you miss so much of the day to day interaction with them.

On one occasion following the transplant I had gone into the bathroom and looked at my reflection in the mirror. I was completely bald; my skin was yellow and so were the whites of my eyes. I came out of the bathroom laughing and one of the nurses saw me and asked, 'what's so funny?' I responded, 'I look like a bloody alien'. She herself then burst out laughing. During my treatment I witnessed quite a few people I had got to know lose their fight. I met some amazing people during my time in and out of hospital, especially fellow patients, their families and friends, doctors, nurses and all the carers and cleaners that keep our health service going. As I consider the support and interactions between patients and families it was amazing, I believe it was due to the positive outlooks everyone generally had and a common bond of fighting together against a life-threatening illness, that there was a sense of community and if one of the patients did lose their fight it affected everyone but there was a level of emotional support for the whole family from the other patients and families and especially the staff that had been on the journey with them throughout.

I was in the RVI when the final results for my degree course were published. One of my university friends went to look on the results board and rang me to say she was there standing in front of the board and said 'Yes your name is on here and you have passed, you have a 2:1 in History with Honours. There were whoops of joy on the ward at the RVI that day, I had achieved it. In the following November I was well enough to attend the ceremony for the conferment of degrees. Phil, our four children, my Mum and Stepdad attended with me. As were waiting to cross the road to go to the Town Hall someone shouted 'Auntie Iris' loudly, it was one of the younger students who had been on my course. She and the other students were really pleased to see me. Being young she said, 'I thought I might never see you again'. When I walked onto the stage to collect my degree there was a loud cheer from backstage from my fellow students. In the evening Phil and I went to the ball I wore a beautiful ball gown and my wig. It was the last time I wore the wig. Jools Holland was the main entertainment and some students were dancing on the tables as he and his band played. Unfortunately, I was far too tired to do that, I would have if I could have mustered the energy, it had been a long day for me, so Phil decided we needed to leave quite early.

There had been a funny incident with the wig. We had taken the children and my Mum and Stepdad to Blackpool for the weekend. As we hadn't been on holiday all year we decided to take them to see the illuminations. We had been in an indoor market and a lady demonstrating a hair accessory asked if I would allow her to use it on my hair to demonstrate. I politely said 'No' but she persevered with me as no one else in the crowd would do it. Eventually, through gritted teeth I said 'it's a wig, it will come off' I am bald underneath the wig, she looked quite shocked. We went into a fish and chip restaurant for dinner following this and when we came out it was extremely windy as it often is in Blackpool. Suddenly my wig blew off and up the road, Phil was then chasing the wig up the road and kept trying to stamp on it to stop it moving. It looked like he was chasing after a rat and trying to stamp on it. We were all in shrieks of laughter especially due to a couple who had seen the whole thing, they were standing there opened mouthed. My youngest child wrote in a literacy lesson about her funniest moment there it was on the classroom wall for all to see; 'The Day Mums Wig Blew Off'. She had gone into great detail as she remembered it clearly, it was hilarious other parents read it after I pointed it out to them and they were laughing too. The teacher informed me that she had been a little concerned about putting it up but knew me well enough to know that I wouldn't mind.

Chapter Twelve

Rebuilding Normality

After I finally returned home from the RVI our lives slowly adapted to me being at home full time, I still became very tired if I did too much and I wasn't very good at pacing myself, so some days I would have to sleep during the day but gradually over time I became stronger also gradually over time the check-ups reduced from weekly to fortnightly, monthly, every three months, every six months and then an annual check-up and they remain so even now. I still take medication but that is nothing compared to the huge amounts that I was initially taking. I didn't take life for granted from the day that I was diagnosed, I learned that life can change in the blink of an eye, you cannot control some things. The Christmas after I had completed all my treatments I paid a visit to the local garden centre and bought some new Christmas ornaments hoping that I would still be there the following year to put them on the tree. For the first few years and as time goes on you still have times when you worry about it coming back but it does lessen and then you discover that you never really think about it until you have to go for the annual check-up and you see patients at the beginning of their treatments. That makes you realise just how far you have progressed and hope that the patients you see recover. It certainly changes how you approach life and I valued even more the extra time that I had been gifted to be with my children, family and friends.

Phil completed his Lay Reader training and became an important member of the laity taking services in place of the Vicar, writing and delivering sermons, leading prayers, administering communion and leading Christian teaching courses. We continued, as we had for years having quiet time in bed each evening doing a daily reading and said prayers together. Our family was very much a part of the church community. We also joined the local amateur dramatics group that rehearsed and performed at the Church Hall. We now had an even larger circle of Christian friends in the surrounding area. Life was returning to normal whatever normal is, the children also had many friends and participated in many activities in the local area and were all doing well at school.

During my second year at university, before I had been diagnosed with leukaemia I had applied to become a teacher. By the time I was interviewed at the University of Durham I had not only been diagnosed I had undergone some treatment and wore a wig to the interview. Phil drove me there as I wasn't well enough to drive myself. The interview was a breeze, I wasn't nervous at all I think this was because part of me didn't believe that I would be going on the course ever but thought it was better to go through the process, I was delighted to be offered a place though. I had spoken on the telephone prior to attending the interview with someone from the admissions department and had explained my position.

She had been very helpful and had explained to me that I could, if successful defer for a year if I was too ill to join the course. I said that I was concerned about whether I should inform the person interviewing me or not, she advised me not to. I did have to defer for a year as I was still too weak to cope with the pace of the course, having to travel up to Durham each day and having to do teaching practises that would also be long days. Durham University is a great place to study, the city is wonderful I often walked into the city during the lunch break, it only took about ten minutes from the School of Education. The university is like Oxford and Cambridge a collegiate system, I applied to Hilde Bede College and was accepted to that college. The course was very intensive but very enjoyable too I did both of my teaching practises on Teesside, the first one at Dormanstown Primary and the final one at Ings Farm Primary School in Redcar, I learned a great deal in those lovely schools during that year and successfully completed my PGCE and became a teacher. To say that I have loved teaching children during my career especially those that find it difficult to learn would be an understatement. The foundation for teaching children and young people who had learning difficulties had been set when I was fifteen when I volunteered at the MENCAP youth club and my interest grew further as a parent volunteer and during my early days as a teacher. Eventually I might even write a book about my experience to encourage other women. to get an education whatever age they are.

Working full time as a teacher was very difficult and tiring but it allowed me to finally build a career and also be at home during the school holidays with the children, I always went into school early and left early so that I would be at home shortly after the children had arrived at home I would then cook dinner and complete any other paperwork that I needed to do before the following day later in the evening. Everything was going well with our lives, my health had virtually returned to pre-transplant, we had more disposable income available to go out and about and we took family holidays to Texas, Colorado, and also in Europe, we even travelled down to Lake Guarda in Italy one year stopping off in Germany on the way there and back, we also went to Centre Parcs and of course many different places in the UK in our caravan. The children especially remember the caravan holidays, visiting different countries and places in the UK including London, playing board games in the evenings, all this enabled them to have a broader education of the world than either Phil and I had received as children. We did many other things frequently as a family besides going to church. We all supported Middlesbrough Football Club and had season tickets and even went to the supporter's club meetings although our eldest son preferred rugby and did decide that he didn't want to go to the football games all the time. We were also able to and bought each other and the children more expensive gifts for Christmas and birthdays. One Christmas I bought Phil a racing bike, it had taken me ages to save up for it out of my salary without him knowing. Friends had stored it in their garage until Christmas Eve when it was smuggled into our garage whilst he was out. Our hard work over the years I believed had paid off, we were able to spend quality time with our four children and each other we were finally reaping the awards after all the sacrifices we had made in our youth. We had been through some life changing moments and everything appeared to be calm.

Two years after my bone marrow transplant we celebrated our fortieth birthdays with a big party. It was good to be fit and well and still be together as a family. Three years later we celebrated 25 years of marriage with a special meal for immediate family and our best man and bridesmaids attended. We also had another party at home for our close friends. Phil's work colleagues bought a bouquet of silver wedding balloons and gave them to him as a surprise at work. He was really pleased with this gift and was beaming when he returned home with them. We had been through a great deal together over 28 years of being together since being fifteen-year olds. We also had a special family holiday as our children were getting older, we realised that they would be stopping within a few years as they made their way into the world and went on holiday with friends rather than family.

We didn't stop studying though. Phil, was studying for a Master's Degree in Business Studies his company funded him in doing this, it would enable him to be promoted further. As a new teacher I had continued my studies as this was expected and would also would enable me to apply for promotions. At the time that Phil was studying for his Master's degree I was also studying for a Master's Degree in Education we both passed these degrees at the same time I graduated in the November and he graduated a few weeks later in the December. A close friend came to my degree ceremony with us and as we were driving home Phil said in a condescending manner 'what's next then a PHD?' I felt like crying it was the way he had spat the comment at me in front of this friend, she looked shocked and she related that to me several days later. She said that she was very proud of me and he should be too. He had humiliated me about something that was a very special achievement why he thought that was appropriate I still cannot understand. I was very proud of Phil passing his Master's, but he was so derogatory about me passing mine and had done this in front of another person too. It had taken me three years of part time studying as well as working fulltime to gain this qualification that would enhance my CV some of the studying was completed during the working day as it was pertinent to my role in the school.

The company Phil worked for had been a huge employer for many years but unfortunately, they started to sell off parts of it. When the section of the company that Phil worked for was being sold off, we threw a farewell party at our house for everyone who worked in the office. It was a very stressful time, Phil searched and applied for jobs away from Teesside and even sought advice from friends. He had informed one of our friends that he did not want to work away from home after he had applied for a position in Cumbria. When she had said that working away from home was not always a good idea as people could be tempted to have extra marital affairs, he was adamant that he would not do this to his family, he didn't inform her that he had previous experience of doing this. The section of the company that Phil worked for was however purchased

by another company and after checking the new con-
tract he had been offered he transferred to that company.
We didn't need to move from Teesside and that meant
stability for all of us. His new role however meant him
travelling to Clitheroe for meetings and he would often
stay over in Clitheroe rather than driving both ways in
one day, he would also say that he had a morning
meeting as well the following day, before needing to be
back in the office in Teesside.

During the period of me recovering from my treatment
and Phil's job insecurity, Ann phoned me and said that
she had found a lump in her breast. We discussed this,
and I advised her to ring the doctor for an emergency
appointment, she did this and saw the GP, she was
referred for an appointment with the breast clinic but
hadn't heard anything for over a week, it had been a
bank holiday during this time. Ann was obviously
worried, I informed her to phone the GP surgery as one
of my friends had found a lump in her breast which was
a cyst, but she had been dealt with very quickly. What
had happened was the letter was still waiting to be sent
in an out tray. This was then sorted very quickly. Ann
had the tests but was unfortunately diagnosed with
breast cancer. She recovered very well after having a
mastectomy. George also became very ill with cancer
but despite having most of a lung removed and further
treatment he didn't recover as well as Ann had done.
One Saturday I drove Phil and I down to Chesterfield to
see Ann and George. Phil drove the car on the return
journey but was extremely quiet. He had been a little
distracted for a few weeks, but I had initially put it
down to his Dad being so ill, but I also had a sneaking
suspicion that there was something else too. When I had

put his washing away I noticed in his underwear drawer the school photo of me taken when I was fifteen that he had always carried in the front of his wallet. I really didn't want to believe that he was having an affair again, but sometimes his behaviour was very bizarre and caused me some concern. He had promised he would never do that again I told myself, he was a Lay Reader now, we were still doing all the family activities together and he was still telling me that he loved me, he was still hugging and kissing me in front of the kids and we were being told to 'get a room' by them. All our normal routines were the same. He had not come to bed at the same time as me and was on his laptop one night which was unusual, when I had gone down to see if he was coming to bed. One night when he was in Clitheroe I had been speaking to him on the phone when I heard a door closing which I had thought was in his room, he informed me that it had been a door outside in the corridor. All of this played on my mind and I didn't sleep very well that night following the visit to see Ann and George. At about 7am I had had enough of tossing and turning with all these thoughts going through my mind. I got up and tried to access his mobile phone, he had a password on it. Why would he have a password on his phone? That was it, I wanted answers I woke him up and told him to turn his phone on. He said, 'can't this wait?' I said 'No'. He got up and turned the phone on but as a message came through he snatched it out of my hands. At that point I knew, and I shouted at him 'You are having an affair.' He just looked at me and then put his head down, he couldn't maintain eye contact with me. It all made sense then. Even though I was shocked I shouted at him and said, 'that is it you b***** you are so out of here'. This situation was so different to when he had the previous affair that I had found out about. We had four children, but they were older and independent other than finances. Having been through leukaemia and a bone marrow transplant had also made me a stronger person too. There was no way I was putting up with this treatment by him again. I went upstairs and began packing his things in cases. When in the process of doing this, I saw the Rotary watch that I had bought him from the prize money that I had been awarded with in my second year at university. It had a black face and a diamond at the 12. At University as soon as I had been given my prize money I had gone into a jeweller's shop and bought that watch for him, wrapped it up and given it him that very same night. I hadn't spent this money on myself or the children I had spent it on him. I thought 'you absolute ****, I went without things for years for you, I even stayed with you after you had cheated on me when I was pregnant and when we had a new born son. He was always saying that we had to be careful with money, that we couldn't afford things. It was only because my salary paid for furniture, clothes for all the family including him, university fees for our eldest child, my car, birthday and Christmas presents that we got any of those things. He had even been saving money in his own name for years including being in a share scheme at work at the expense of me not being able to save in my own name. He must have been spending money on the other woman instead of his family. Angry is not even a way to describe how I felt at that point, I picked up the watch and took it downstairs I then placed it carefully onto the kitchen worktop and got the rolling pin out of a kitchen drawer. Phil was stood there in front of the sink drinking coffee but watching me but when I lifted the rolling pin into the air he said, 'Oh no!' I have never been so angry in my life, I hit the watch with the rolling pin and the face of the watch broke I continued to hit it and bits of watch flew all over the place. I shouted some things at him about having sex with the other woman as I did it and then leaving the watch and the rolling pin on the worktop I got some bin bags out of a cupboard and walked out of the kitchen back upstairs and packed the rest of his clothes in the bags. He was so lucky I didn't hit him with the rolling pin. I then put all of the suitcases and bin bags into his car, he had a company car by this time; a Ford Galaxy. I was also devastated as well as being angry and rang a close friend, she came around immediately. He was just about to climb into his car when she arrived, he said to her; 'Stuart wouldn't have done this to you would he?' Her husband, had been killed in a helicopter crash the previous year. How dare he compare himself with someone who loved his family worked away, had never cheated on them and had tragically died.

That afternoon I rang a friend who worked part time for an accountant and knew a solicitor. She gave me the name of the solicitor and the following morning I rang the solicitor, he made me an appointment for that day and informed me what paperwork to bring with me including any financial information, I filed for divorce that day due to his adultery. It was a few weeks until I found out the other woman's name; I have named her Laura in this book. Phil appeared shocked, hurt and became very angry about me filing for divorce, he told me and others that he did not want a divorce, he even told our friends and his mother Ann, 'loads of men do this, Iris should put up with it', really? My response to this was 'not to me they don't, he had a chance after our youngest son had been born. He became even more arrogant as our finances were being discussed, and bullied me by ringing me up a great deal threatening not to give me any money, that he would turn our children against me. The constant phone calls led me to frequently putting the receiver in the hall drawer and turning off my mobile, this meant I had no way of receiving calls from friends or family. One evening a friend was at my house when he rang, he wanted to speak to Hannah who wasn't at home. I informed him that I would ask her to call him when she returned home, I then put the phone down due to him shouting at me. The phone rang again as soon as I had walked into the living room, I said 'that will be him again' my friend answered it, Phil had already started shouting down the phone, but he stopped when she informed him it wasn't me that it was her and she would ask Hannah to call him when she returned. On one occasion when Phil visited me he stood in our dining room and informed me that if I took half of his pension then he would take half of mine. Really? I thought is he totally stupid. By this time, I had six years' worth of a teacher's pension, he had over twenty years of his company pension My response to him was 'you can have half of my pension it is work f*"^ all'. This was not the response he obviously expected from me he looked both astounded and furious that I had finally stood up to him on the finances, he had always controlled all our finances even when I was working I would check with him before I made purchases of items other than groceries. Also, I was doing the household accounts now and despite having less income each month we were managing very well, that was a very interesting process. During the divorce financial settlement, following legal advice, I continued to stand firm on the pensions being split, it was now the law that pensions were split. Prior to the year 2000 many women had lost all rights to their husbands pensions on divorce and this was causing financial difficulties for many women especially those that had remained at home to raise children. The government recognised this and became more insistent on pension sharing in divorce settlements and made pension sharing law. Phil's salary at that time was three times mine when his bonuses and other benefits were considered, he would still accrue more pension than me following the divorce, he also had the share scheme that he had and was still paying into. On joining the teaching profession, I was given the opportunity to pay a one-off lump sum payment, it was about £4,000, into the teachers' pension fund, this would enhance my pension fund. Phil and George looked at it and both decided that it would be better not to pay a lump sum out of our savings and informed me that I would be okay as I would be secure as Phil had a very good pension fund and if he died I would still be taken care of through his fund. His whole demeaner and attitude was that I should be subservient to him in the divorce settlement as I had been regarding finances and other areas throughout our marriage, he had always had the final say on things. George had telephoned me a few times and given me financial advice as he volunteered for Citizens Advice. He gave me Phil's address in Darlington when I said that I didn't know where he was living. Despite George being so ill he hadn't been to visit him for a few weeks and of course that meant the children hadn't seen their Grandad either, so I took them to see him. My eldest son remarked that I had been kind to them. I always was and am kind to people and respectful, kindness and respect costs nothing and elderly people should always be respected. George even agreed to go to the hospice one day a week to give Ann a break after I had spoken to him about it. I had said to him that he could meet other people with cancer and receive support from the McMillan Nurses. It is very scary having cancer and must be more so when you know it is terminal. George was worried about leaving Ann alone after he passed away, they had been married since Ann was 19 years old. He rang me the evening before he passed away, but I was out until late with friends and thought he would be in bed by then, so I didn't get to speak to him to find out what he wanted to speak to me about and Ann didn't know either, it was probably just another call to see if I was okay. It is wonderful that one of my Grandsons has his name as his middle name.

On a few occasions I had discussed the divorce with Laura's husband; when I said to him that she had attended the court and even went into the room to discuss the finances with the solicitor and barrister he replied 'yes, she would, she knows exactly what she is doing, she has done it before'. He also said a few more things that I won't repeat. He informed me that their son would not have anything to do with her anymore. Phil had informed me and my solicitor that she was of 'limited means', he had informed me that she worked part time as a receptionist at a doctor's surgery and that he had met her when she was at the surgeries Christmas party that was at the same place as his Christmas party in Clitheroe. This wasn't true, he lied about her occupation, my solicitor had informed me that things often come to light many years later and that cases can be referred to appropriate legal authorities. Several years later I discovered that Laura's occupation had been in the financial sector, her husband's statement about her knowing what she was doing made sense. Making false financial statements in a divorce is a criminal offence but even though things do come to light later it is still a difficult choice whether to pursue them or not especially when you have children as it can lead to a custodial sentence. Phil attempted to have a clause put into the divorce settlement stating that I had to remain living in the home that we had shared, his solicitor was contacted and told in no uncertain terms that was imprisonment, and was not allowed. Why he believed that he could continue to control my life and my movements was incredible. There was no way I could remain in that house under his instruction and even more so after he had been in the garage and removed items such as a wheelbarrow after the divorce settlement, the police directed him to return it.

During the time of the breakup and divorce things were very difficult for myself and our children. My GP signed me off work and prescribed me antidepressants. I did return to work only to be sent home again after the Rector of the Church of England School where I worked came to my classroom to speak to me, the staff at the school were very concerned about my health and wellbeing. I broke down in tears as I informed him about the threats Phil had made to me on the telephone the previous evening.

When I visited the GP, who was the one who had given me the diagnosis of leukaemia a few years previously so knew me well, he persuaded me to see a counsellor. He said I know you are a strong lady, but this is far too much to cope with. When I had my first appointment with her she said 'I am going to read your referral from your GP, it read 'I have had to twist Iris' arm up her back to see you...' I talked to her about my past and everything Phil had done previously including the affair that I had known about. One night Phil called me and cried down the phone saying that he had broken up with Laura as he didn't want a divorce. He decided to see the counsellor with me. He met with the counsellor by himself one week instead of me going for my appointment then the following week we attended my appointment together. He had attempted to blame my childhood for his behaviour the previous week but wasn't clear about which aspect of my childhood he had meant when the counsellor discussed what had been said the previous week by him, he came across as being confused, I don't think he expected my counsellor to discuss what he had said when I wasn't present. My childhood was in fact to blame for me putting up with his previous behaviours, I wanted a stable family life for myself and our children. He then attempted to justify the affair he claimed it was because one of our children had a messy bedroom, how many teenagers have messy bedrooms? Also, that another of our teenagers and I argued too much, isn't that what teenagers do? Don't they know everything and push the boundaries? Isn't it the parent's role and responsibility to keep boundaries in place? Another reason was that I bought him shirts, how naughty of me daring to buy him some shirts, I also bought him jumpers, pants and socks but that must have been okay, it was just the shirts caused him to have an affair! Another bizarre reason that he plucked out of the air was that we got a puppy, he had always had a dog when he was growing up and agreed to our children having a dog. When asked why he had the affair when I was pregnant, he said it was because I had become pregnant, I felt like hitting him at that moment and shouted at him that we had sat down and discussed having another child and I asked him why we had then gone on to have a fourth baby; Jonathan and then Hannah after losing Jonathan. He couldn't give an answer to this at all and remained silent. He hadn't said that in his letter to me, he had said that he had wanted each of our children, although he did of course state Satan had made him do it on that occasion. He didn't tell the counsellor it was due to Satan. Looking back, I find it difficult to understand why he would initiate discussions about having another child unless as some friends have expressed their thoughts that Phil was happy when I was tied to the house looking after small children but then resented it later once the children were older and I could do other things. Honestly, what such pathetic reasons to break up a family especially when he was also telling people that he didn't want a divorce. He obviously didn't dare say that he wanted to have sex with other women as well as me which is what he was implying when he had informed our friends and his own mother 'loads of men do it and that I should put up with it'. He never explained why Satan got in there again 16 years later, you would have thought he would have had more awareness of Satan especially being a lay reader and teaching people how to avoid Satan getting in there. After all he had said that God had healed him of that part of him.

To say that their behaviour during the divorce was inappropriate is an understatement. Laura always accompanied him to court, I don't know what she was trying to prove. Did she think he was a trophy that she had won? She hadn't won anything I had thrown him out, I was divorcing him on the grounds of adultery. Was she attempting to take control and dictate what the settlement would be? On occasions, my friends and family that witnessed such things did have a giggle about it with me. He had never really taken responsibility for his behaviour over his previous affair or taken on board how much that had hurt me. On one occasion following his first affair that I had found out about, I informed him that what he had done was worse than what even Jack and Sheila had done to me. His response to that was "Yes, I am a right F**** B*****" I didn't disagree with him. At that time people had told me that a leopard never changes its spots, but I didn't listen. I wanted to do everything I could to keep our family together to ensure that our children had a stable family life and I achieved that until they were young adults.

Phil had pretended to be a Family man and a Christian to a great deal of people, before you challenge me on that statement, as a Lay Reader he was dressed up as a leader of the church he wore a cassock and surplus with a blue scarf to demonstrate that he was teaching the ways of God to people of all ages and was advising them how to pray and prayed with them. Meanwhile he was leading a life that was far from being a Christian. He was committing adultery not for the first time either but again. He had said it was Satan the first time who got in and made him do it. I don't think so, I think some men just can't help it, if it is offered on a plate they take it. According to Phil through the statements he made to others, loads of men think having extra marital affairs is acceptable. I am so glad I kept those letters following his first affair. What did he really mean? Had it been a way of manipulating me on that occasion? Telling me he regretted it, he wouldn't do it again? One of our friends, a very wise lady informed me that she had spoken to Phil and her conclusion was that he was a person that decompartmentalised his life, that he had a compartment that contained myself and the children, his home life, another compartment contained his work life another his church life and then another one contained his life with other women. When the home, work and church life came together it was fine they were compatible but of course the one containing the other women was not compatible with any of the others and that is when there is a huge conflict. It all sounds far too complicated to me and people like that cannot keep it up indefinitely. Why pretend to be someone you are not? It must be very stressful. Doing some research on this I have discovered that in many cases the 'other' woman eventually makes more demands on the man and will even go to great lengths to get rid of the wife, her rival, and even let the wife know of the affair in various ways, she doesn't have any loyalty to the man's wife or children and she doesn't care in the least about the destruction her inappropriate behaviour causes she doesn't see it as her problem, it is the man's problem. Her aim is to win the battle to prove that she is the better person. This is quite bizarre behaviour to me. A man or a woman that will cheat on a long-standing partner and ultimately destroy their children's security is not a prize at all, and the woman is certainly not better than the wife. To me it seems even worse when a woman does this to her own children. Even woman who suffer domestic abuse protect their own children by first trying to appease the man to keep the family together and then end up taking her children to a place of safety.

Our children were obviously devastated on the breakup of the marriage but have also been quite strong as I had to be when my Mum and Dad split up and I do feel sorry for them. Phil and I had been together when my Mum and Dad separated and divorced, he had seen the effect it had on me at the time and afterwards, he knew how his Mum felt about people having extra marital affairs. We had discussed marriage breakups over the years from the break-up of my Mum and Dads marriage and then over the years as people we knew divorced and we had both agreed we would make our marriage work. Phil was frequently telling me that I was his best friend. It had not been in our plans at all for our family's future and certainly not mine. In fact, that is why I put up with Phil's behaviour regarding his first affair. We wanted for our children what I hadn't had but what Phil and his sister had experienced, two parents being side by side supporting their children. Hopefully they and their partners will do the right thing and value their marriages and what that entails and 'exclude all others....' And not allow Satan to 'get in'. My sons are both parents now, they share the childcare with their wives including the daily routines of feeding and changing the children.

It was difficult for my children when I sold the family home but the three eldest were either at University or about to go. It was impossible to continue to live there for several reasons. There was a great deal of gossip about the breakup of the marriage due to Phil having such a high-profile role in the Parish. Although I did have a network of friends that supported me as much as they could. Quite a few people outside that network of friends thought it appropriate to try to initiate conversations about the situation with me by saying things like 'I could not believe it when I heard, I thought you were the perfect family....' The Vicar even spoke to me and said that he could not believe it, that he had attended evensong that Phil had lead the previous Sunday, and that he had chatted to Phil about me and the family, he said that you wouldn't have thought there was anything wrong at all. He also informed me that he had rang Phil on several occasions, but Phil had refused to meet with him and then wouldn't answer his phone when he called him. When the new Vicar arrived in the Parish she wanted to meet with me. I met with her and she then informed me that she had checked if he was still listed as a Lay Reader and that he was. She informed York diocese about what he had done, and they had removed him as a Lay Reader, she had got him struck off. There was no way I could remain living in that Parish or the house as Phil had invaded my privacy far too many times in different ways. He even stated that 'he didn't feel like it was his home anymore as I had redecorated the house. Hello, it wasn't his home anymore.

Chapter Thirteen

Unknown Sisters

Having a sister or sisters that you have never met is not unique but is unusual. Until I moved to Jack and Sheila's I didn't even know they existed. John had always missed Shirley especially and Sheila continually said that Shirley and Margaret would be returning to live with us all. Shirley and Margaret (Maggie) lived together in the Harrogate area and had been fostered by a couple but their Dad sadly passed away. Their Mum was an intelligent and educated lady who became a teacher and Head teacher. It was due to this that she knew how to fight to keep her daughters with her. Hazel their Mum fought to keep them and won.

Maggie had only been a few months old when she had been taken into care due to the cruelty and neglect she and our older siblings had suffered. She had been hospitalised upon the point of going into care. Maggie didn't go to live with Shirley immediately after being discharged from hospital, she lived in a children's home and later went to live with Hazel following Shirley repeatedly asking for John to be brought to live with them. When Hazel enquired about John being able to be fostered by her and her husband she was informed that he was already happy and settled with foster parents and it was thought best to leave him there.

When I was living in Texas it was a great surprise to hear that Shirley and Margaret had contacted our birth family. They had obviously, like anyone would, wanted to know the truth about their past for themselves. It can be confusing over the years when other people appear to know or supposedly know more about your past than you do. John had met them on one occasion during the time the rest of us were living at Sheffield Road with Jack and Sheila when they were teenagers, the meeting had been arranged by social services and they said that they had wanted to see him again but that they did not want to meet Jack or Sheila, just John.

Six years after my other siblings and Jack and Sheila had met Shirley and whilst Phil and I were still married I met Shirley for the first time. Following the meeting in Chesterfield with Jack and Sheila and my siblings Shirley did not want to see Jack or Sheila again but she did remain in contact with John, Ken, May and Irene. Shirley now lived in Devon with her husband and son, we went to Devon on holiday in our caravan, we had four children by now, the youngest being just a few months old. I was quite apprehensive, what do you say to a sister that you have never met? What would she think of me and my family? May had informed me that she was alright as were her husband and son. We found the house where Shirley lived and got out of the car. She must have been looking out for the car as she walked around the corner of the house to come down the path to meet us as soon as we arrived. My heart stopped beating for a moment, May hadn't informed me that Shirley was the absolute double of Sheila to look at. I took a deep breath and we hugged each other but I think we were both a little apprehensive. Fortunately, Shirley was not like Sheila to speak to, she had a very 'well spoken' voice and her husband was very lovely making us feel welcome and organising activities for the children. Geoff and Shirley had a boat and went fishing a great deal, Geoff thought that the children would like crabbing. We followed them to the local garage and Geoff bought the children crabbing lines and bait; bacon. We then we drove to a nearby estuary as the tide was out, Geoff and his son Malcolm showed the children how to use the crabbing lines the children loved catching the small crabs and putting them into their buckets. They didn't like releasing the crabs afterwards though, I think they thought they would be able to take them home and keep them as pets. We met up with them following day again and talked about our pasts. Shirley asked me many questions about Jack and Sheila I was asked what had happened when I lived with Jack and Sheila and what they were like. I related to them what it had been like and why I had left. They appeared to be pleased with the responses and said that is what both May and John had said. They, I think, had found the descriptions given by May and John unbelievable of our collective and individual experiences of living with Jack and Sheila. No one wants to believe that the people who have created you could be so cruel, that they would neglect their children from birth and continue to physically and emotionally abuse their children. You don't want to be associated with them at all, you do not have any pride about the family that you were born into only shame. It takes a long time to realise that it was not your fault that you were born into those circumstances and to have the strength to fight it by being a better person, in fact the best person you can be so that you have self-worth, pride in yourself, your achievements and that others are also proud of your achievements. Due to Shirley remaining with her Mum, Hazel she achieved a great deal. Shirley had music lessons which enabled her to be part of a famous band, Ivy Bensons All Girl Band and she travelled to many different countries playing with the band before meeting Geoff, marrying and becoming a mother. We continued to be in contact but maybe not as much as we would have been if we had been brought up together. Shirley played the big caring sister part very well when I needed support, she rang almost every day when I was ill and often spoke to my Mum. Unfortunately, Shirley was diagnosed with multiple sclerosis around the time that I had leukaemia and over the following years became more infirm. She never changed though she remained as kind hearted throughout her illness and maintained her sense of humour. Unfortunately, Shirley passed away suddenly almost two months ago as I write this. John, May, Irene, Robert and I travelled down to attend her funeral together. The time we had with her was limited but at least we did have those precious times with her and will be able to carry those memories of being with her with us.

It was more difficult meeting Maggie I didn't meet her until nine years after first meeting Shirley. Maggie had unfortunately suffered a major breakdown and had been placed in a hospital. We finally met when Shirley thought that Maggie would be well enough to cope with meeting me. Maggie lived in Ripon which was only about a forty-minute drive away from where I was living on Teesside. I went to meet her by myself the first time I met her. It was amazing that I had been to Ripon previously and had driven down her road and parked just around the corner from her bedsit, so near but so far! I met Maggie at her bedsit. She had a look of Sheila in that she had the same black wiry curly hair. Her build was more like Jacks and she walked like him, probably due to her being overweight. We went to the British Legion Club that she frequented and I was introduced to some of her friends there. I have never been a big drinker or visited pubs regularly. The first time I got drunk was an accident, I was thirty years old, and people kept refilling my glass before I had emptied it I wasn't aware of how much I had drunk, well that is my excuse, I was sick and then had a huge hangover the next day. The room spinning is an awful sensation, I don't understand why anyone would want to be in that state. It has happened a couple of times since, both accidental that is my story and I am sticking to it. Anyway, the meeting with Maggie was very different to the one that I had experienced with Shirley. I spent a few hours in the pub with her and her friends and then said goodbye. On that initial meeting I think Maggie felt safer with her friends being with her. A few weeks later after speaking to Maggie on the phone a few times, May and I along with my youngest daughter collected Maggie from her bedsit and took her out into the countryside near Harrogate to a pub that Maggie chose for a meal. May had met Maggie previously and Maggie appeared to be more at ease at this second meeting, it was much better for me too as we weren't sat in a club with lots of strangers to me that were drinking pint after pint of beer. We had a lovely time and we took photographs of us together so that Maggie could also have copies to keep. We went into the bedsit afterwards and it was in quite a state. Maggie was still having counselling sessions and couldn't work due to her mental health issues, she didn't have much money to buy things for the bedsit. May being the kind of person that she is visited Maggie again with her husband Mick and decided that they should sort out Maggie's bedsit. Mick is very talented at DIY and has his own business. Phil and I helped too and before long Maggie's bedsit was a changed place, new flooring, newly decorated throughout and new built in cupboards to store everything. Maggie had chosen the colour schemes and was delighted with it. We held a reunion at our house on Teesside, John, Ken, Irene, May, Maggie and I of course, Shirley lived too far away to attend. Our children were all there too, Maggie didn't have any of her own, she had been married but was divorced, that was one of the reasons for her breakdown. She had a lovely time with all the nephews and nieces and her siblings and all of us with her, like Shirley she was well spoken and had the same sense of humour as the rest of us which was becoming more apparent the more time that we spent with her.

Seven years after meeting, Maggie was working in a hospital and loved it, her mental health was much improved. On a Sunday morning I received a phone call at home, May and Mick were staying with my new husband that weekend. Maggie had been found dead at home. Maggie had not been well and had been in hospital but not as we were aware diagnosed with any-thing. During the night she had obviously got up to go to the toilet and had suffered a brain haemorrhage and had died immediately. The post- mortem revealed this and that she had cancer that was quite extensive, she must have known about the cancer but didn't inform anyone. What made her death more tragic at the age of 51 was that she had moved on with her life so much. She was not only working but had moved into a nice bungalow, had bought herself a car and had surplus cash that she used to buy herself nice things.

Maggie as I have stated was divorced, without children but had not written a will. Writing a will is so impor-tant but so many people just don't do it. Due to not having a will, Maggie died intestate so her next of kin was Jack. John visited him and informed Jack that Maggie's affairs would need sorting, bills needed to be paid including the funeral. Jack immediately said he wasn't paying any bills. He signed Maggie's affairs over to her siblings to sort out. John, May and I did this, it was a very difficult thing to do in that we had to decide what to throw away, send to charity shops etc.

Robert one of our younger brothers brought Jack to Maggie's funeral in Harrogate. Eric, Hazels second husband explained to the mourners what the timetable and running order of the funeral was, he also stated that there would be a collection in Maggie's memory in aid of the NSPCC. At that point Jack shouted, 'well that is one organisation that I won't be giving to, that Coxon took my kids of me'. He had no conscience at all, he took no responsibility that it was due to his and Sheila's cruelty and neglect that had led to his children being taken into care under a Place of Safety order and their subsequent custodial sentences. I was so cross with him and had begun to march up to him when someone whispered 'Iris, stop'. I still don't know who that was but it held me back.

We all went into the crematorium and then Eric came up to me and asked if I and my siblings wanted to walk behind Maggie's coffin as she would soon be arriving from the funeral home. I called my individual siblings by name and said, 'come with me', I didn't invite Jack to join us as Hazel didn't want him to. We were waiting for Maggie to arrive when Mick came rushing into the room and took Robert outside. Jack had been mouthing off in the crematorium. Some of Maggie's favourite music was being played and Jack made a very loud comment about one of the tracks being played being 'a joke'. This was totally inappropriate, my youngest daughter said later after I had asked her what she thought about her Grandfather, she replied 'he is a knob, he doesn't even know how to behave at his own daughter's funeral when her favourite songs are being played'.

When Maggie arrived, the floral tributes were being put onto her coffin when May spotted a bouquet from Jack it said something along the lines of; I will love and miss you always, Dad. We just looked at each other. During the funeral I did the eulogy, my brothers and sisters had made contributions which I put together and they approved it. Robert, Mick, John and Ken were on hand in case Jack started any trouble, they were going to remove him from the crematorium if he started to kick off again. Although it was difficult, I managed to do the eulogy without any interference from Jack. He left almost immediately after the funeral, Robert got him away from us as soon as he could.

After the funeral service and during the wake the undertaker asked May and I what we wanted to happen to the floral tributes. They were to go to Hazel and Eric's as Maggie's ashes were to be scattered in their garden where she had loved to play. However, we didn't want Hazel to see Jack's floral tribute so asked the undertaker to throw those in the bin so that Hazel wouldn't be upset. The undertaker said that he had never been asked to throw a floral tribute in the bin, we said 'you don't know Jack and what he did to Maggie.' After the Wake we went to Pately Bridge to Hazel and Eric's and had a cup of tea with them. Hazel was still upset at Jack's outbursts at the funeral, she referred to him as 'the father'. The undertaker delivered the floral tributes whilst we were still there, Hazel went to look at them and said, 'the father's flowers are not here', May and I told her that we didn't think she had seen them earlier and had asked the undertaker to bin them as we didn't think she would want them in her house, she agreed she hadn't wanted them in her house.

It is sad that we only knew Maggie for a short time but hopefully she was happy that she had met all her siblings and got to know them and their families before she died. Although she was still receiving support when I had initially met her I think Mick, May, Phil and I sorting out her bedsit helped her too.

Chapter Fourteen

The End of Life

When Sheila my birth mother passed away, this was about three years before Maggie passed away, I received a phone call to tell me that she had died and that when the funeral was arranged they would ring me to let me know. How did I feel about this news? A little confused I didn't know how I was supposed to feel. Should I feel upset? Should I be crying? Should I feel pleased that the woman who had been imprisoned for child cruelty and neglect and then gone on to beat my siblings and I with canes, not nurtured, fed or clothed us had died? She wouldn't hurt anymore children for sure and hadn't been able to for a long time as she had been on oxygen for most of the time and had been in and out of hospital according to my brother John who had visited her in hospital. I didn't feel anything other than oh she has died, it wasn't even like finding out that a neighbour had died, and you could say 'oh that's a shame he or she was such a nice person'. I couldn't say anything nice about her at all, and certainly wouldn't be missing her in anyway.

A friend was at my house at the time and so was Phil, we were separated at this time, but he was visiting me, he said that he would go with me to the funeral I said that I hadn't even decided if I wanted to go. He then said to my friend that really, I was upset about it, I was just hiding my feelings. It was amazing that he believed that he could read my mind. He had always been very good at telling me how I felt about things. He really didn't get it at all. I didn't like the woman and although she had given birth to me, that was it. She had been the egg donor and incubator and Jack the sperm donor. My Mum was the Mum that he knew, she was very much alive as was my Dad. Not this other person. If you think about it, I had only been under the same roof as them for eight years at the most when you consider me being in care and then being at my home in Maltby during the school holidays it wasn't even a full eight years. Some days even when I lived under the same roof I didn't see her for more than a few minutes as she was still in bed when I went to school and I was out in the evenings or in my room.

May didn't go to the funeral neither did Shirley or Maggie but I finally decided to go. Jack was there on the front pew, he looked like a doddery old man. The vicar spoke about Sheila and said that she had been a good mother, he obviously hadn't been told about the physical abuse, the mental abuse or neglect of her children or serving a prison sentence for child cruelty and neglect. The vicar also said that she had been a good grandmother, she hadn't even met my children. Jack had put the phone down on me when I called to say that some of my children wanted to meet her after I had sent her a letter asking if she would meet them but that I didn't want to see Jack. Vicars of course can only say what they have been told about the deceased person.

When we came out of the crematorium my brothers John and Ken, my sister Irene and I stood together they were trying to persuade me to go back to the house for a cup of tea. John and Irene reassured me that they had spent days cleaning the house and Irene said that she had used lots of bleach on everything but not to go upstairs or use the toilet upstairs. My sister Irene then noticed my brother John's wife also called Irene was crying. Irene said to John's Irene 'why are you crying?' Irene replied, 'because not one of her children has cried at her funeral, how sad that not one of her children have cried about her dying'. We pointed out to her that not all her children were even there.

I did go back to the house and we all stayed in the kitchen chatting. I hadn't seen my brother Tommy for quite a few years we spent quite a while chatting and caught up on what we had been doing. Jack didn't come into the kitchen, he didn't make any effort to speak to us at the funeral or acknowledge us being there but then again, I didn't make any effort with him either. Robert and his wife had stayed in the living room with Jack so before I left I went in to say good bye to them. Jack made no response at all.

I haven't changed my opinion about Sheila or Jack at all. I firmly believe that some people are evil, she made a conscious decision whether to be nice or not towards her children, the hate was in was in her eyes when she beat her children for no reason and when she decided to scare us by locking us in the cellar. She had never made any contact with us when we were in care and didn't attend arranged meetings. She never made any effort to comfort or reassure us when we had been taken away from our Mums, if she had then that would have included making sure we could attend to our basic needs. For me personally attending her funeral drew a line under that part of my life especially seeing Jack as an old man. The fear I had of him had gone.

About eighteen months after Sheila died I received a phone call at home, it was my step sister Ann, she was crying but managed to tell me that my Dad had died. I couldn't believe it; how could he have died? He had been in and out of hospital for the past few years as he had emphysema due to having been a coal face worker in the coal mine and smoking most of his life. He had to have oxygen everyday (he still smoked though) but he hadn't been in hospital and I had only spoken to my Dad and Joyce the day before, I spoke to them every day. She explained that he had collapsed at home and the paramedics had been called, this had happened several times before. This time though they couldn't save him he had died probably before he reached the hospital. It was devastating I cried, I screamed I don't think my children knew what to do with me. I could not believe that I would never be able to speak or see my Dad again. I drove down to see Joyce the next day and the following days, if I was with Joyce then I was closer to my Dad. Once my Dad had been taken to the undertakers and could be visited I went to see him, that made it real for me and broke my heart. I went to see my Mum after I had seen my Dad, when I walked through the door she said, 'are you all right' and then said, 'of course you are not'. I broke down and while she hugged me I clung onto her and said, 'you had better not die or I will kill you'. The things you say when you are distressed!

Joyce included me in the meeting with the funeral director and when the vicar came to discuss the funeral service. Remembering what had been said about Sheila I still had a bee in my bonnet about the Vicar not knowing the person and then not telling the truth about the deceased person I asked if I could do the eulogy for my Dad. Joyce said that I could. I wrote it including bits of information given to me by Joyce and others and Joyce had the final approval. It was hard doing it in the service, but I was doing it for my Dad. My Dad had always said that he would be there at Hannah's first show in London when she became a famous singer, so she sang 'Somewhere over the Rainbow' at her Grandad's funeral although after a while she looked down to the floor. She told me weeks later that it was because her Grandad was sat next to me when she was singing. Hannah also said that he visited her a few weeks later at home and asked her to look after me. She said she hadn't been frightened so I suppose that is okay.

Joyce passed away after my Dad, that was very sad. Joyce and I had developed a lovely relationship I continued to speak to her every day after my Dad had died. Joyce had experienced some of the things that I had and supported me a great deal. She had lost a baby and understood how I felt about losing Jonathan. When my Dad was in hospital, her daughter or son in law would take her down to the hospital late morning and she sat with him all day making sure that he ate and drank, Dad had lost most of his vision by then and so she was worried that he wouldn't be able to see the cup of tea or the meal. On one occasion Dad and Joyce ended being in the hospital at the same time and the lovely hospital staff moved them to bed spaces next to each other so that they could still be together.

Albert, my stepdad was then admitted into hospital to have an operation to remove a growth from his kidney. He was recovering quite well but the night before he was released I noticed that he had a bit of cough developing and informed Sheila (my sister in law) who was staying with Mum again after I had given her a few days off during my half term. Sheila took Mum to visit Albert the following day and was informed that he could go home, so after a wait for his medications which included some antibiotics and sorting out getting Mum into her wheelchair and to the car and then Albert to the car they went home. Albert however collapsed on the doorstep Sheila managed to get him into the bungalow and into his bed. Over the next few days no one visited from the health centre to change Alberts dressing. Sheila rang them, they hadn't been informed that Albert had been discharged, the nurse on seeing Albert arranged for the Doctor to pay Albert a home visit, the antibiotics were not for the cough that he had or the chest infection that he had developed. Albert was gradually getting worse but wouldn't entertain going back into hospital. The Doctor made visits to see Albert and by the end of the week Albert was back in hospital he was so ill he no longer had a choice in the matter. Albert agreed to be sedated, that would hopefully give his body the rest that would help him recover. Unfortunately, he wasn't getting any better and ended up in intensive care on life support. Sadly, after several days Mum had to make the decision about switching off his life support, the medical staff had tried to remove the support, but Albert hadn't responded. We were all with him, including his brother, it was the most bizarre, awful but calm experience that I have ever been part of. The hospital staff explained what would happen once the machine was turned off and asked if we wanted the machine on silent, we chose silent. The process began and we all sat with Albert as each of the monitors went from wavy lines to the final flat line they have when the patient has died. It seems surreal, the person is still there but not breathing with the assistance of the machine anymore it all happened in a very short time, a few minutes. Looking back, I think we were all shocked it all had happened so quickly everyone went into the 'what we need to do' mode that happens after someone dies.

Albert had been a big part of my life. Although I had been angry about his affair with my Mum he had looked after her. Albert had lost his one an only child a son Paul, he would have been about my age, he had died on the operating table when he was having a brain tumour removed, he was only about six years old bless him. He had been a lovely Grandad to my children, my youngest daughter had him wrapped around her little finger. When Mum and Albert stayed at our house he always bought them a packet of sweets when he bought his newspaper each morning. Albert had also supported me and my family in many ways. He didn't have to bring my Mum up to my home every other week to help her look after my children, Phil and our home when I was ill. They even made all the meals including Mum making Phil a packed lunch ever day with a neatly folded-up napkin (piece of kitchen roll) which was of great amusement to Phil. Albert didn't have to support me throughout my divorce. He once gave me an envelope with a substantial amount of money in it during that difficult time so that I could pay someone to decorate the hall stairs and landing, I made him take it back. My brother in law did it free of charge, he wouldn't take the money, so I just bought the paint myself it had been a lovely gesture I informed him that if I needed it in the future I knew that I could ask him for it. He could be a pain too, he liked to have everything as perfect as my Mum did, so if he made comments that 'this needs doing, that needs doing....' I used to say, 'well you know where the tools are'. We had needed a clothes post putting up for years, the line was tied to the fence, not good when you have a family of six people and there was always masses of washing. One of the jobs Phil was 'going' to do Albert sorted it out for us, he went to the DIY shop and bought a clothes line pole and cement. He could also say things that perhaps he should have thought about and the impact they could potentially have on me. One day when I was visiting Mum and Albert he explained that they had received a letter from Phil. Albert was very angry about it especially the contents of it. Phil had acknowledged that they probably would be upset with him but believed that it was in my best interest that we separated. This was hilarious, I had kicked him out and was divorcing him not the other way around. Even now I cannot think why he wrote them such a letter was he attempting to gain some form of control of me through my family? It was a little creepy in a way. He also hoped they could be friends again. 'My Mum had refused to read it and when I asked her why she hadn't read it, she replied 'I don't want to read anything that bastard has written.' Wow, my Mum had not only sworn she had used a different 'b' word this time. Albert and my Mum then informed me about when they had stayed at my house during the time I was in hospital and how Phil had taken one of our babysitters that I considered to be a friend home in the car and was gone for hours even though she only lived within a few minutes of our house. He never took her home when I was at home. One of my older Christian friends knew the person and said that she wouldn't be surprised, as the person in question had done a similar thing with another local family after I had asked her about it. This was mind blowing, whilst I had been fighting for my life he may have been having an affair. When I asked Albert and my Mum why they hadn't told me about it before they said it was because I had been ill and then he appeared to have settled down again. In some ways I wish they hadn't told me at all. My Mum also said that she thought that everything Phil had been and was doing was to make me ill again, commit suicide, or bring back the leukaemia, I reassured her that he wouldn't make me commit suicide or make the leukaemia come back. They both said that they also thought that I had been through enough during my lifetime and that they would never forgive him for what he had done. They said that they had treated him like a son (Mum even made Phil an egg custard when we visited them, or they visited us as it was a favourite of his), they said he had repaid them by lying to them as well as me and our children. They were furious with him for the way he had treated me and our children, they were also livid with him for daring to send them a letter where he was trying to minimise what he had done so that they would eventually be his friend and welcome him back into the family even though he was being vile towards me. He obviously didn't know that I spoke to them and my Dad and Joyce every day. Albert gave me the letter to keep so I stored it with other letters he sent. I missed Albert after he died for the person he was and the part he had played in my life and yes, I did the eulogy at his funeral too.

Mum as her mother before her had both osteo and rheumatoid arthritis, she used to call it Old Arthur. She always appeared to cope with it quite well and took the numerous medications that she had been prescribed. There was no way that she could be left in the bungalow to look after herself. Sheila had stayed most of the time that Albert was in hospital and I had stayed during the half term week. By the Thursday I was ready to batter her. I rang Sheila up, she said 'is she organising you?' Organising me? She was wondering around all the time and picking things up, wrapping everything in carrier bags and when I threw one of the carrier bags of rubbish in the bin outside she got cross, 'you never do things right girl, you have to put the carrier bag of rubbish in the kitchen bin bag and then put that in the bin'. Oops, I really messed up! When Albert had died it was as though she didn't really understand. Mum couldn't sort her own medication out and gradually we realised it wasn't just about being able to open the packaging.

Before and after Albert died we had begun to realise that there was something more than 'Old Arthur' going on but Sheila thought that it was down to her missing and being worried about Albert when he was in hospital and then because he had died I had to agree with that thought. Anyway, Mum agreed to live in sheltered accommodation in Maltby and the bungalow was put up for sale. She had a lovely ground floor one bedroomed flat with her own front door she still had some privacy and independence. She had only lived in the sheltered accommodation a few weeks when Mums GP rang Sheila to say that he had sent Mum into a local care home, Mum had opened the main door wearing only a half-slip (an underskirt) and this apparently hadn't been the first time that she had done it. During the time that she was in the care home, Mum continued with some strange behaviour including not eating but hiding food inside napkins and appearing to get very muddled. Sheila was managing everything and made sure that Mum had a visitor on the days that she didn't go across to Maltby. She also quizzed the staff about Mums care and her obviously losing weight, they informed her that they didn't have a battery for the sit on weighing scales. Sheila took Mum for all her appointments and on one day I went to see the GP with them I managed to get into the room before Mum and said 'I know you cannot discuss her with me, but we are worried as she is hiding food and the only conversations you get with her are about the past or yes and no answers'. He arranged for a test to be done on Mum after asking her a few questions during her appointment. I was there when the initial test was done Mum couldn't answer the questions or even draw a clock face properly. After this Mum was formally diagnosed with Alzheimer after Sheila took her for a more detailed test in Rotherham, at least it all made sense now; the way my Mum had spoken to me over the carrier bag and bin bag was not how she would normally speak. She was no longer as chatty as she always had been. She had fooled everyone by always speaking about the past and nodding or agreeing with what was being said this meant when we all thought that she was joining in family conversations she hadn't been. Alzheimer's is a cruel disease, it slowly takes away the person in mind and it can also change the person's personality. Following a period of being in hospital for a chest infection, Mum was moved to another care home in Maltby as we were not happy with the first one that she had been put in and Sheila continued to organise that Mum had at least one family member visiting her every day. Mum was much happier there and Sheila had organised for a landline to be put in Mums room so that we could call her. Mum also had a mobile phone, she didn't get on very well with that, by the time she managed to answer it the call had gone to voicemail and Mum no matter how many times she was shown how to use the phone could not remember due to Alzheimer's.

Mum had been into hospital a few times with her chest and although she was very ill she always perked up when anyone visited, she never moaned. One of her life-long mottos was 'there is always someone worse off than you'. She would also point and say, 'that poor old lady there isn't very well you know.' They were probably younger than her! Once she was well enough she would get out of her bed and walk across to them to have a chat. The last time she went into hospital it was different, she wasn't getting any better and was much quieter than usual. On the Saturday Mike and I had gone to visit her she was asleep most of the time but when Mike had gone to the toilet she said to me 'I have enough of this'. I asked her 'enough of what'. She replied in a determined voice 'this'. I said to her 'are you wanting to leave us'. She didn't reply so I said to her 'if you are wanting to leave us then you need to go to sleep and rest', that short conversation was very emotional for me. On the Sunday we got a phone call from Sheila to say we needed to go back to the hospital as the doctors were wanting to stop Mums medication, they had said that it wasn't working, Ronnie had challenged this and said to the young doctor 'are you sure' the doctor said that Mum would remain on the medication until the following day when the Consultant would be back on the ward. Mum was asleep most of the time again. Ronnie decided to stay overnight with her and I returned home to Shropshire as I hadn't taken any over-night things with me but would return the next day, I didn't sleep very well that night. The following morning, I drove back and arrived at the hospital early. Sheila was already there Ronnie had gone home to get some rest. The doctor came to see Mum and spoke to Sheila and I. He was under no doubt at all that the medication was not working and taking Mum off it was the best thing to do. We asked him if we should get Ronnie back and he replied 'yes' so Ronnie was called to come back to the hospital. Mum had been brought up a Catholic and even though she hadn't practised her faith for many years I thought that she ought to have the last rites. The nurses arranged for the hospital Chaplin to visit Mum. Even though she wasn't conscious he did the ritual and I joined in the prayers that I knew. I also rang my eldest son Daniel who is a vicar just in case the catholic priest didn't make it. Within just a few hours Mum passed away peacefully in her sleep with Ronnie, Sheila, Daniel and I by her side.

To say that my Mum's death was hard is putting it mildly the death of your Mum should I suppose be one of the hardest losses to deal with. Well she may not have given birth to me in the natural way, but she gave birth to me by taking me from Oakwood Grange Children's Home and loving and caring for me as a Mum should do, she gave me new life. When we were separated during the school terms it was difficult, but they were only short periods of time. Six weeks is usually the longest half term but that sometimes felt like so much longer, this was forever. On social media sites people post things about which person who has died would you like to speak to again, hold again, see again. Well My Mum would be the top of my list.

Chapter Fifteen

Finding Out the Truth

Years later after leaving Jack and Sheila's, May and I carried out some research into our past at Rotherham Library we found an article about Jack and Sheila being sent to prison for child cruelty and neglect we also read the court transcripts about the trial. The court transcripts revealed that Jack had been in prison previously for larceny. Jack and Sheila were not married at the time of the trial, he was still married to someone else. We decided that we wanted to find out more and May thought she could remember the house where Auntie Doris, one of Jack's sisters lived. Dinnington isn't far from Rotherham so off we went in search of Jack's sister. We drove to Dinnington, May looked out for landmarks that she could remember. May knew it wasn't far from the church, once that was found we quickly found the house. There was a man building a wall I asked him if a Doris White lived there he said no, but the lady who did live there came out. I explained that we were looking for Doris White, she said she had lived there but now lived around the corner. We drove around the corner and May knocked on the door Auntie Doris answered the door and was delighted to see us. We, including my youngest daughter Hannah were invited in and the kettle was put on immediately, a typical Yorkshire welcome.

Auntie Doris was quite elderly and chatted away while she made the tea she appeared very excited. She told us that her daughter Maureen who May had known had passed away due to having cancer, she said how much she missed her. There were photos around the room of her children and grandchildren of whom she was obviously very proud as she informed us who they were and what they were like. The table had a nice clean tablecloth on and everything in the house was pristine. She informed us that she had seen Jack and Sheila a few months ago and that Sheila wasn't well and was on oxygen all the time. We explained that we didn't have any contact with them but that we had been to Rotherham Library and had found the newspaper articles about Jack and Sheila being sent to prison. Auntie Doris said that she wouldn't say anything bad about Jack as he was her brother. Then as many old people do she began to tell us what had happened. She explained that she had been to the house in Thurcroft and cleaned it, but they didn't keep it clean after she had cleaned it for them and that when she had her own babies she didn't have the time to travel to Thurcroft from Dinnington anymore to clean their house as well as her own. She called Sheila a lazy dirty bitch, she was still affected by it all and became a little tearful and apologised that she hadn't been able to stop it from happening. Auntie Doris asked how John, Shirley, Ken and Margaret were and was pleased when we updated her about them.

We then asked her about when we had gone into care as we had been taken into care from her house, we had our notes by now and knew that we hadn't been taken into care from Carlisle Terrace. Auntie Doris then explained that Jack and Sheila had been evicted from 6 Carlisle Terrace and had turned up on her doorstep with four children, May, myself, Irene and Tommy (in age order). She then got upset and said she would have loved to have kept us, but she couldn't as there wasn't room for us as well as her own family. Auntie Doris then forgot what she had said about not saying anything about Jack and explained that he stayed in bed all day and that he didn't even get up to go to the bathroom let alone work and that Sheila would take him a milk bottle for him to pee into and they were then left lined up on the window sill. Again, she called Sheila a lazy dirty bitch for not emptying them, she didn't call Jack lazy. She said that Sheila didn't help with anything at all and so she, Auntie Doris ended up looking after us as well as her own family. Her husband and herself decided that they had to decide and informed Jack and Sheila that they would have to find somewhere else to live or put us into care. That is what Jack and Sheila did they put all four of us into care. May said that she remembered a baby being on the front seat being held by a lady and Auntie Doris agreed that it would have been Tommy. She got upset again as she informed us that when the car pulled away Jack and Sheila began laughing and messing about pushing and shoving each other. She said, 'you wouldn't think their children had just been taken off them, we were disgusted with them'. We also asked about Jacks first marriage, but she wasn't forth coming with much information about it but did agree there had been a daughter and thought that she lived in Manchester. I have tried to find Jack's first marriage but haven't been able to do so and have not been able to trace my half-sister either we think her name is Josephine so if anyone knows a Josephine whose birth father was called John Francis Allcock please get in contact. Auntie Doris was pleased to see us and gave us a great deal of information some of which we know especially about Jack and Sheila being lazy, dirty and uncaring. She also told us about her other brothers and sisters and said they were lovely, we knew that about some of them as the ones that we had met were just like her too.

Receiving our care notes enabled us to discover how Jack and Sheila managed to persuade social services to give us back to them. That was a huge question that had puzzled us for years especially as John, Shirley, Ken and Maggie had been removed and a court order made. Maggie's care notes were more detailed than ours too and she had been given a great deal more verbal information by her social worker as had Shirley due to them remaining in care until they were young adults. Jack and Sheila had moved away from Dinnington to Chesterfield and initially lived in the old bus but were then provided with a small house on Mill Street in Chesterfield on the edge of the town centre. This house was not appropriate for us to be returned to either. Sheila then wrote to the People newspaper to get the publicity to threaten Chesterfield council into rehousing them. She also wrote to the Queen! Chesterfield council were reluctant to rehouse them due to Jacks appalling historical work record and the reluctance of both of them to maintain a home in a clean state. Social services also had some reservations about us being returned to them but as May, Irene and I had not been removed as John, Shirley, Ken and Maggie had been social services didn't have the same powers to prevent it. Correspondence from Chesterfield council stated that they were proposing to transfer them to a larger house, but not to force Rotherham Social Services to return us to their care. The houses on the street they were living on were due for demolition for anticipated road improvements.

When children are in the care of the local authority the parents are expected to contribute financially to their children's care. Jack and Sheila had not made any contributions to our care and were in fact in arrears to a very substantial amount due to having seven children in care. A caseworker from the Sheffield Family Service Unit became involved and he was persuaded by Sheila that she wanted us back, he made a huge impact on enabling Jack and Sheila to have the return of their children. He persuaded Social Services to write off the debt as there was no possibility of Jack and Sheila ever paying it off but had said that Jack would inform them if he was working so that he could make some contributions, this was never going to happen as they had three more younger children by that time. Jack was employed by this time, but he didn't work for more than a few weeks at a time even though they were continually demanding that we were returned to them. When he was working of course he was even then keeping a good proportion of his earnings for his own gratification and not purchasing the items for the house such as bedding and furniture that they would need if we were to return to them. When Jack discovered that John was working a statement about Jack was made that he appeared to be more interested in his (John's) early discharge than in resuming care of the younger and dependent members of his family.' So, this grown man who had hardly worked throughout his life wanted his fifteen-year-old son returned to him so that he could work and bring money into the house. This is what he wanted all along, for his children to work and keep him so that he could continue his lazy lifestyle. The caseworker from the Sheffield Family Services Unit even found them furniture and then asked West Riding County Council to provide bedding so that we could be returned to them. Our foster parents, our Mums and Dads had provided all those items for us and more, but our birth parents were not prepared to do it? On discovering this I found it unbelievable but there it was in black and white. As I have already stated Shirley and Maggie were never returned. Their Mum, Hazel, met with Miss Short and she assured Hazel that she would not support any return of Shirley or Margaret. So, if it wasn't in Shirley and Maggie's best interests to be returned to them why was it deemed to be in our best interests? The social workers knew that Jack was lazy, bombastic and aggressive and had always failed in his duty as a husband and father and that Sheila was failing as a mother even with three children. She was not keeping these children clean or the house and the notes mention that the three children were very naughty especially Tommy.

When people speak about nature or nurture I will stand on the side of nurture. If a child is valued and loved, then s/he will also value and love. Below is a poem that I have displayed in most of my classrooms when I was teaching:

CHILDREN LEARN WHAT THEY LIVE

Dorothy Law Nolte

If a child lives with criticism,
he learns to condemn.

If a child lives with hostility,
he learns to fight.
If a child lives with fear,
he learns to be apprehensive.
If a child lives with pity,
he learns to feel sorry for himself.
If a child lives with ridicule,
he learns to be shy.
If a child lives with jealousy,
he learns what envy is.
If a child lives with shame,
he learns to feel guilty.
If a child lives with encouragement,
he learns to be confident.
If a child lives with tolerance,
he learns to be patient.
If a child lives with praise,
he learns to be appreciative.
If a child lives with acceptance,
he learns to love.
If a child lives with approval,
he learns to like himself.
If a child lives with recognition,
he learns that it is good to have a goal.
If a child lives with sharing,
he learns about generosity.
If a child lives with honesty and fairness,
he learns what truth and justice are.
If a child lives with security,
he learns to have faith in himself and in those about him.

If a child lives with friendliness,
he learns that the world is a nice place in which to live.
If you live with serenity,
your child will live with peace of mind.

With what is your child living?

I feel very blessed to have been raised within a family that lived by those words and not by a family that were the opposite. As for Jack he passed away and not in the best circumstances. My youngest birth brother, removed Jack from his three-bedroomed house that was fitted with a stair lift, had a downstairs toilet to his two-bedroomed house that he shared with a 22-year-old girl, their baby son and her son from a previous relationship. The house did not have a downstairs toilet or a stair lift. Jack ended up going into a care home and had to be showered twice due to the state he was in. Then due to being so ill he spent some time in hospital before returning to the care home. At the age of 89 Jack passed away during the night alone. My youngest daughter stated at the time of his death that he deserved it after what he had done to us, it was Karma. Even though he was a dreadful father he was apparently a good grandfather, Irene has informed me of some of the nice times that she and her daughter experienced with him as have nieces. John, Ken, Robert, Irene and I attended his funeral and on what would have been his 90th birthday we scattered his and Sheila's ashes together at one of their favourite places.

Chapter Sixteen

Freedom from Control

Any marriage breakup must be stressful especially when you have been betrayed and you cannot see a future as the future that you were expecting has been stolen from you. The stress is immense and is there 24/7 but the other party does not have any sympathy or compassion they have moved on with their life.

Following the breakup of my marriage to Phil, the Deputy Headteacher at the school where I was teaching decided that it was in my best interest to move on by starting to date as her friend had done. Dating as an adult was a very scary proposition, I had never had this experience. Anyway, Angela who was a very bright and bubbly person was insistent that this was the way forward, so I decided to give it a try and if I found out that it wasn't for me, then there was nothing lost. Angela gave me instructions from her friend about dating sites and my youngest daughter helped me set up a page. It was a very interesting process and quite a few men contacted me, some were nice, some were weird too. I met one man and had a drink with him but he worked at the same company as Phil so that was a non-starter. After a week or so Mike popped up as a match and a friend looked at his profile and said that I should message him. After a while I met Mike and it turned out that he knew my sister Irene as he had worked for the same company as her when I was also living in Chesterfield. When I returned home from that meeting I called Irene, she remembered Mike and said that he was a nice person and that I should be safe with him. We continued to see each other, Mike's ex in laws also gave him a good reference as did some of his long-term friends. The rest is history as they say. When we married my Mum was there as were many of our family and friends, my youngest son gave me away although he did say in his speech that he had tried to sell me on eBay! We have seven children between us and as time has gone on we also have sons and daughter in laws and grandchildren.

Overall our life together has been calm and we have dealt with the loss of loved ones and illnesses together. We have had some lovely holidays in the UK and abroad and have ticked off places on my bucket list including swimming on the Great Barrier Reef and visiting Uluru.

Phil for some strange reason decided to send Mike a letter and a copy of a letter that he had sent me. He has been very good at sending letters over the years attempting to justify his behaviour and making false promises. He basically informed me that he had said some horrendous things to our children about me. Why would he do that? He had obviously threatened on several occasions to turn our children against me during the financial settlement period and that was what stressed me out so much. He could not just accept that there were consequences for his behaviour and that I had any rights to a financial settlement. Mike was not interested in anything that Phil said about me and did not read the letter or email, he gave me the letter which I stored. The envelope was handwritten by someone else and not Phil I wonder who did that? There have been other incidents over the years where Laura has caused upset to mine Phil's children that they have complained to me and others about. She caused my eldest daughter to be in tears on her wedding day. This resulted in me taking her back to the bridal suite with her husband before the end of the evening. Laura even complained that she wasn't in enough wedding photographs! Her constant complaining in line waiting to have graduation photographs taken upset my youngest son, he ended up not having the formal photos taken at his degree ceremony this was after he had studied medicine for five years. His wife has the formal photographs taken the same day and it is very sad that they cannot display their individual photographs of them graduating with the same degrees on the same day, they had met at University but were not in a relationship at that time, it would be something special to have on show in their home. She also refused to allow Phil sit at the top table at our youngest son's wedding after he had already agreed to. I was informed by my son that I would be sat with the bride's father and Phil with the bride's mother. Mike would be sat during the meal with other members of my family. Then I received a phone call and my son informed me that I would be sitting on the top table with Mike as his Dad wasn't allowed to be on the top table. The bride's father sat with his ex-wife, his wife didn't cause a fuss at all in fact she did exactly what would be expected and remained in the background but helped with some practical things to help the couple. That is what I have done at each of my stepchildren's weddings, kept in the background. It is their day and their parent's day and I have always been delighted to be invited to such special occasions as Mike was to my children's weddings.

Laura's daughter, who didn't even know me posted some inappropriate and inaccurate statements on social media about me on the day my first grandchild was born. One of the vile things she stated was that I wouldn't know what it was like to have to have proper parents as my real parents had given me away. She also threatened me, but I don't suppose you could expect anything else from someone like that really. I can only think that she had received some misinformation from Phil about me, maybe he thought he had to try and justify what he had done to his wife and children, but I don't think that he liked the fact that he did not have the moral high ground in this, I had it. He could have just stuck to his original reason that Satan had made him do it, that it was out of his control. Amazingly I had paid for the gift that my youngest daughter bought her unborn baby as Hannah had spent all her allowance. I had felt sorry for her being a single mum and thought how hard that must be. Phil attempting to defame my character to cover his inappropriate behaviour, was shocking and hateful and that is one of the reasons that I decided to write the facts in a book, it is 'My Life and My Story' to tell certainly not someone like Phil, or anyone else. I am not perfect, no one is (my Mum taught me that) but I do not deliberately hurt people. My early experiences are why I have always since being a teenager given my time freely in helping people in fulfilling their potential. It is why I became a teacher of Special Educational Needs. It is why I have never committed adultery. My children all know who fathered them and were brought up by their birth father and mother within an extended family until they were young adults. Of course, I kept copies of what she had written, and I did write to her. Everything I had been through had made me stronger and I was not going to accept this from someone I did not know. This is the letter I sent her;

Dear Toni

This letter is in response to the inappropriate statements that you have made about me on Facebook which is as I stated a public forum. Since you have written these statements you have made libellous statements against me. You have included Phil, Laura and mine and Phil's children especially Hannah who was extremely upset and cried. You then continued making comments about me on MSN to Hannah which again is a public forum and in written format, these comments upset Hannah even further. You have shown Hannah what kind of a person you are. You should be ashamed of yourself. (She is several years older than Hannah) Hannah may be 18 but she is still growing into adulthood and is as you know currently away from home at University.

I would like to bring the statements that you made on Facebook to your attention.

You responded to comments that were posted to Hannah's wall, these were made by me to my daughter so therefore they had nothing to do with you at all.

They did not refer to you. You therefore had no right to make any comment. The statements were about me becoming a Grandma and Hannah an Auntie for the first time.

Phil got together with your Mum, that also has nothing to do with you. But if you would like access to my medical records you may. There are statements in there made by Phil to the counsellor (that I was made to see by my GP due to the stress Phil and your Mum put me under and due to my previous medical history – acute myeloid leukaemia). Phil stated that he had an affair due to reason's that were not directly due to me it was more to do with family life in general, coping with teenagers etc. Phil always maintained that I had been a good wife and mother. Phil informed friends and family that he did not want a divorce. That 'loads of men do it, Iris should just put up with it'. He also cried down the phone that he did not want a divorce. I chose to divorce him as it was obvious he was unable to remain faithful, your Mum was not his first affair. These things happen and both Phil and I have moved on with our lives.

You may think what you want of me. You do not know me at all. However, *you should not be saying inappropriate things about me openly, this is slander, you should not be recording it in writing that is libellous.*

She made inappropriate comments about my children saying that they had said things about me. I checked this with my children and informed her; *My children have not said that about me, they are not like that and I should know. Phil and I brought them up to be nice, polite and caring people.*

She stated; 'U wouldn't know what it is like to have proper parents would u! Didn't ur real parents give u away!' After saying that I didn't know how to be a proper parent. This was a terrible thing to say and I responded; *You do not know the facts about my childhood, how could you? How would you define a 'proper parent?' Just because someone isn't brought up by people that are not their birth parents, it doesn't mean that they don't learn how to be parents. I had fantastic foster parents, and my upbringing was excellent, they are my Mum and Dad. Phil thought a great deal of my parents and they of him. My Mum and Dad separated when I was 17, it is difficult when that happens. Phil knew all of this as we were together from being 15 and he was a great support to me during that period in my life as were Ann and George. This all made me more determined that our children wouldn't go through this and that is why I put up with Phil's previous affairs and other things, I know that you are not with your daughter's father so are you going to tar her with the same brush? As I have said how do you define 'proper parents?' Are they the people that are your biological parents or the people that bring you up?* Her making such statements about my Mum and Dad was insulting to my Mum and Dad and indeed all my foster family. Also, to all the wonderful foster and adoptive parents out there and of course other people that have also been in the care system.

She said that my kids were great. *I agree mine and Phil's children are lovely. Phil and I have been blessed with children that have grown into fantastic beautiful young people. They are academically bright, successful and will no doubt have further successes in life, the world is their oyster. That is nothing to do with you and indeed your Mum. Phil and I are their biological parents, we brought them up.* She was trying to infer that her Mum had done more for my children! She didn't meet them until they were teenagers and older! Neither her Mum were there when I gave birth to any of my children or when I was up during the night breast-feeding and changing them. When I looked after them day to day including when they were ill and taught them how to interact with others, read, write, cook, wash, iron. Looking after them when their father was 'away on business'.

No, I doubt that you would see an apology as appropriate.

Sad? I don't think so what have I got to be sad about? I have four beautiful, successful, loving children, a beautiful daughter-in-law who has just given birth to my first grandchild who is absolutely beautiful and is blessed with two parents that will always put her needs first.

Lying? No, I don't know what you mean. If you wish to expand on this, then please do so in writing. I don't lie and cheat what is the point? You get caught out eventually and people never trust you again. She never informed me what she meant, it must have been libellous to write it.

Hate? I doubt that Phil or Laura hate me, they have no cause to. Quite frankly it shows your immaturity and what a nasty minded person you are to say such a thing about them.

Everyone knows what I am like! Really? Would you like to expand on this, inform me who has said what? I could also give you some of my contacts so that you may also go and interview them to find out what people think of me. Many have known me since my childhood. Amazingly she never responded to that either.

I do nothing for my kids? Just where do you get that from? I have always put my children first. We all have opportunities to have affairs. I just declined as I didn't want to put my children through that or Phil even though he had done it. Unfortunately, some people do not value the family in the same way as me. Your family was broken apart that was not my fault. You may be angry, but you have no right to vent your anger on me involve my children, nor do you have the right to involve your Mum or Phil in trying to score points against me or whatever your pathetic immature brain appears to lead you to do. She was again implying I did nothing for my children. How she came to that conclusion I do not know.

Give it out? Take it? I will not have you or anyone else make slanderous or libellous statements against me in such a public way even more so when they involve my children.

Bad word? What bad word was that? Are you threatening me? What with? Please clarify so that I may take the necessary action to protect myself and my family.

If you have the capacity to take this on board then listen carefully, If you ever make any more libellous or slanderous comments about me in the future then I will take the necessary legal action against you.

Meanwhile I expect you to apologize in writing to me, my children especially Hannah, Phil and your Mum.' She didn't of course. I haven't had any further trouble from her. In a way I feel sorry for her that she is so full of hatred.

Chapter Seventeen

The Future

Four years after marrying Mike I was diagnosed with breast cancer Mike was a rock, despite him not having any experience of my previous illness he had lost his own Mum to cancer. He attended all my follow up checks and took me for my daily treatment (radiotherapy) in Leeds and cared for me after the invasive investigation I had to undergo. At that time, we lived to the east of York, so it was at least an hour's drive each way to the hospital in Leeds. My daughters also helped by taking me for some of my treatments to give Mike a break from the daily driving. My youngest daughter came with Mike and I for the results of the type and level of cancer it was. Fortunately, it had been caught early and after five years I passed the checks and I remain in good health.

We moved to Shropshire a few years ago as Mike changed jobs but are now hoping to move back north as we have both retired early. Mike's Dad has passed away now, so we don't have any strong ties to keep us here and our children and grandchildren although scattered around most of them live in and around Yorkshire and the other sets of parents live around there too so it makes it easier for them to see everyone. Finally, I am in a relationship that is based on mutual trust and respect, we share everything equally. Mike has been away on business on several occasions and I have had no doubts when he was away at all that he was 100% faithful. Mike doesn't control me in anyway, in fact no one does I am free to speak to anyone, spend money on whatever I want but it is usually on our children and grandchildren especially buying fabrics and making them unique items.

In York and here in Shropshire I have made some lovely friends and am looking forward to spending time with my friends in and around Teesside once we move north and for friends to visit us our new home.

None of us knows what the future holds for us especially how much time we have left, but what I know is that it is not worth spending time with someone that you cannot trust.

If you ever find yourself in similar circumstances to those experienced by me don't give up on yourself, you deserve better. If you think someone is controlling you, then it is them that has the problem not you. Don't let them control you by using your weaknesses, mine was my children and wanting a stable family life for them, to give them what I hadn't had. Even though it is stressful stand up yourself, move on, find something that you have always wanted to do and do it. Go out and meet people build yourself a better life. There are lots of nice, honest, kind people out there. Some of my friends that were supportive of me during Phil's affairs and the breakup of the marriage shared their thoughts about his control of me; that it was fine when I was at home with babies and children, but he didn't like it when I proved myself to be on his level academically by gaining qualifications, they had seen it years before I had realised. I found that very sad, but I think there is some truth in it. After I had gained my qualifications I began to stand up to him on things such as ungrounding our son after I had grounded him, he wasn't there when the grounding had been implemented as a final straw for misbehaviour, Phil was undermining me instead of informing our son to behave or sitting down to discuss it together. It was my role to set boundaries for our children, that is why they are well behaved. Well most of the time! Now as I look back it is bizarre that I put up with all of this controlling behaviour, it is tantamount to emotional abuse. People that knew me then no doubt have seen the changes in me over the years and those that know me now will probably say that I am a strong woman and 'feisty', I trained as a union representative for one of the teaching unions and served on the local association committee and spoke at the annual conference. Unfairness, injustice, bullying and exclusion towards children and adults is wrong and I will take action against it. My MP's secretary said she knows my address when I attended a meeting along with a group called WASPI that I co-ordinate, she was taking addresses to ensure that we were all constituents. I am also a councillor where I live so am involved in making sure issues my fellow residents are concerned about are discussed in the Council meetings and action is taken.

After moving to York, I attended York University and gained another qualification – teaching Mathematics to a higher level than the PGCE had given me. Currently I am still receiving many calls from recruitment companies headhunting for Maths specialists. Mike was proud of me when I passed the course. Mike always says thankyou for every meal that I prepare him as I do him. Everyone should have a Mike by their side, calm, intelligent, loads of common sense, loving, faithful and extremely patient when I am being independent/stubborn, for instance when he wants to help me get something from the top shelf and I insist on getting the step stool to do it myself!

Enjoy the life you have.

Love and Best Wishes

Iris xx

Epilogue

This book has not been easy to write as the process revisited some very traumatic incidents experienced at various stages of my life. There is a tendency to have a negative opinion of children that have been in care. This can be very damaging and prevent them from reaching their potential. My siblings that were also in care have not continued the cycle of deprivation set by our birth parents. We have all worked hard the whole of our lives. We have had to fight the stigma of being born to the wrong people despite only living with them briefly.

My story needed to be told by me due to some people that believed they had the right to use and manipulate my childhood experiences in a negative way to hurt me and justify their own inappropriate behaviour. Fortunately, I have saved many documents that support the truth. The experience has taught me that the most dangerous person in the world is a fake friend.

It is *My Life*, *My Story*.

Lightning Source UK Ltd.
Milton Keynes UK
UKHW01f1830060618
323849UK00001B/15/P

9 781786 231734